PRINTING IN COLONIAL
SPANISH AMERICA

PRINTING IN COLONIAL SPANISH AMERICA

by
HENSLEY C. WOODBRIDGE
and
LAWRENCE S. THOMPSON

Whitston Publishing Company
Troy, New York
1976

Copyright   1976
Hensley C. Woodbridge and Lawrence S. Thompson

Library of Congress Catalog Card Number 75-8384
ISBN   0-87875-076-2
Printed in the United States of America

To Anna and Annie

CONTENTS

PREFACE

In 1962 one of the authors (Mr. Thompson) published his *Printing in Colonial Spanish America*. The present revision is largely the work of Mr. Woodbridge. It is hoped that the bibliographical references provided here will make it more useful than the original work. The authors wish to express their special thanks to Dr. Pedro Grases for many helpful suggestions.

Hensley Woodbridge

Lawrence S. Thompson

ILLUSTRATIONS

Chapter I
part i

THE INTRODUCTION OF PRINTING TO MEXICO

The precise facts about the introduction of printing to most localities are rarely known in full detail,
and the old Spanish colonies are no exception. There
has always been some uncertainty about the beginning
of printing in Mexico, and in recent years there has
been a controversy over this matter almost as violent
as any that ever raged over Johannes Gutenberg. One
thing is certain: Multiple copies of basic religious
works were urgently needed by Spanish friars in their
zeal to win hundreds of thousands of Indians for the
Church of Rome. The exact manner of the implemen-
tation of this fundamental aspect of Spanish imperial
policy is shrouded in some mystery.

Juan de Zumárraga, bishop of Mexico since 1528
(later, in 1547, to become the first archbishop), and
Viceroy Antonio de Mendoza were actively interested
in establishing a press in Mexico.[1] Mendoza, appointed
viceroy in 1530, did not establish his residence in
New Spain until 1535, and it is certain that during
this lustrum he was giving much thought to the tem-

poral needs of his jurisdiction. Zumárraga, who was in the metropolis in 1533 and 1534, undoubtedly conferred with the new viceroy about the spiritual needs of New Spain, and we know that a printing press was in the minds of both men. In the Archivo de Indias in Seville there is a memorandum from Zumárraga emphasizing the need and convenience of a printing press and a paper mill in New Spain. [2] It is altogether likely that about this time Zumárraga began negotiations with Juan Cromberger, the noted printer of Seville, to send a printing press to Mexico. We do not know when and how a press was sent to Mexico, but we only know that one was sent by Cromberger[3] and that there is no positive evidence of the existence of a press in New Spain before 6 May 1538. On this date Zumárraga wrote to the Emperor:

> Poco se puede adelantar en lo de la imprenta por la carestía del papel, que éste dificulta las muchas obras que acá están aparejadas y otras que habrán de nuevo darse a la estampa, pues que se carece de las más necessarias, y de allá son pocas las que vienen. [4]

There is no other documentation to indicate the presence of a press or a printer in New Spain before this date. However, arguments have been advanced forcefully (and rebutted with equal vigor) to prove there was a printing press and a printer in Mexico before 1538 and that he practiced his craft.

In 1953 and 1954 the noted Spanish bibliographer Francisco Vindel published a facsimile and a critical study of a little book entitled *El rezo del Santo Rosario* which he claimed was printed in Mexico between 1532 and 1534. [5] He argued that the book was printed from type from the shop of Juan Varela of

Seville on a small press for printing playing cards
sent over to Mexico with Juan"s son, Pedro, in 1531.
He studied the careers of the Varelas, their economic
position and standing in the printing trade, the business
of printing playing cards in Seville and in Mexico and,
finally, the special devotion of the Dominicans to
propagating the prayer of the rosary in Mexico from
their first arrival there in 1526. Vindel's arguments
in favor of the priority of *El rezo del Santo Rosario*
were forceful, but the evidence was not conclusive.
Even before the *Apéndice* appeared three reputable
Mexican historians issued a rebuttal to Vindel's claims
which was accepted unanimously by the Academia
Mexicana de Historia at its session of 10 August
1953. [6] Vindel immediately came to the defense of his
position with an open letter of eight pages, issued in
Madrid on 10 May 1954. [7] He pointed out deficiencies
in the attack of the Mexicans and summarized his at-
titude toward them with the words "¡¡¡¡UN LIBRO QUE
NO HAN VISTO!!!!", but he added no substantive
evidence to his side of the polemic. In 1956 Vindel
issued a study in which he offered what he considered
conclusive evidence that *El rezo del Santo Rosario*
was printed on "Aztec paper." [8] Vindel's claims have
not yet received generally unqualified support.

There is substantial evidence that a printer was
in New Spain possibly as early as 1536 or even before.
At some time between 28 April 1536 and 1538 the
precentor of the Cathedral of Mexico, Cristóbal de
Pedraza, was in Spain and at that time wrote a memorandum to the king advising "que un maestro imprimidor
tiene voluntad de servir a V. M. con su arte, y pasar
a la Nueva España a empremir allá libros de yglesia
…" [9] Medina thought that one Esteban Martín was this
master printer, that he may have arrived in Mexico as
early as 1534, and that he was at work from 1535 to

1538. It is of considerable interest to note that on 5 September 1539--some sixteen months after Zumárraga complained of the slow progress of printing in Mexico-- there is a record of the acceptance of one Esteban Martín, *impressor,* as a *vecino* of the city of Mexico. [10] It should be noted that final confirmation of the status of *vecindad* usually did not take place until after some years of residence.

If Martín actually printed, not a scrap of anything from his press is known today. Medina and those who accept his ideas about Martín's activities as a printer think that he printed the *Escala spiritual* of San Juan Climaco. Dávila Padilla refers to such a book, al- though he attributes it to Juan Pablos. [11] Alonso Fernández also attributes it to Pablos but assigns to it the specific date of 1535, [12] and González Dávila dates it 1532, the year to which he also assigns, in- correctly, the arrival of Viceroy Mendoza. [13] Medina believed that only Martín could have been the printer of the *Escala spiritual* and offers strong arguments to support this contention. Conclusive evidence is still lacking.

The first printer in Mexico whom we can identify without any equivocation is Juan Pablos, or Giovanni Paoli, a native of Brescia. [14] His arrival in Mexico was preceded by negotiations by Mendoza and Zumárraga with Juan Cromberger, a leading Seville printer, possibly as early as 1535. The press may have been in Mexico as early as 1536, but it is doubtful that it was oper- ated by Pablos (as Dávila Padilla and Alonso Fer- nández state), for the available evidence would suggest that Pablos did not go to Mexico before 1539.

Zumárraga and his associates were eager to get the press in operation and were disappointed by the delays, a fact obvious from his letter of 6 May 1538 (*supra*). They were especially concerned with the

4

problem of printing a catechism in Mexican, and on 2 March 1537 a *Santa Doctrina* in Spanish and Mexican, composed by Juan Ramírez, a Dominican friar, was sent to Cromberger to be printed and bound. [15] Negotiations dragged through the year, and it was decided to send the book back to Mexico, where it could be printed more easily. The last we hear of the work is a note found by León Pinelo in one of the books of the Casa de Contratación: "Fr. Juan Ramírez, de la orden de Sto. Domingo, escribió un libro intitulado *Santa Doctrina*, en lengua castellana y mexicana, el cual se remitió a México para que fuese calificado y examinado, y se volviese para imprimirle. 29 de Enero de 1538." [16]

Several surviving documents tell the story of the trip of Pablos to Mexico, with equipment and assistants. Most famous and enlightening is the long contract of 12 June 1539 between Cromberger and Pablos. [17] Cromberger drove what would seem to have been a rather hard bargain with Pablos. The agreement was to remain in force for ten years. Cromberger agreed to pay transportation to Mexico for Pablos, his wife (Jerónima Gutiérrez or Nuñez), his assistant, Gil Barbero, and a negro slave named Pedro, and also agreed to pay freight charges on equipment and supplies. Cromberger was to furnish paper, ink, and type against requisitions submitted by Pablos one year in advance. Pablos was to print 3,000 sheets a day ("tres mill pliegos"), literally an impossible number from a single press. One can only guess that "mill" was an arithmetical slip by a Seville scribe. Pablos could retain none of the income from the press beyond what he needed for bare living expenses. Further, he could engage in no other business and was to act as sales agent for his principal, but without receiving any commission on such sales. Barbero was to receive a wage of five and a half ducats per month. After a period of ten years, all expenses, including original transportation costs, wages, expenses for subsistance and depreciation of equipment were to be deducted from the profits, and Pablos would receive one-fifth of the net.

There was always a deep-seated professional jealousy and fear of rivals among the early printers of Mexico, a fact of which there is considerable evidence later in the century. Cromberger, scion of a noted and successful family of printers, was fully cognizant of this situation, and therefore he ordered Pablos to melt down old type rather than to sell it at the possible danger of encouraging competition. In addition, all publications were to bear the imprint "en casa de Juan Cromberger."

In addition to this famous contract, there are several other documents which are significant for the story of Juan Pablos' work as the first known Mexican printer. It is of especial interest to note that he was not received as a citizen (*vecino*) until 17 February 1542, [18] thus rendering it most likely that Martín too had to wait two or more years before reaching the same status. There are other documents supplementing the contract between Cromberger and Pablos, including Pablos' receipt to Cromberger for equipment and expenses, [19] the contract between Cromberger and Gil Barbero under which the latter was to work in the new Mexican printing shop for three years, [20] and Cromberger's power of attorney given to Pablos on 4 July 1540. [21] Further documents such as those recording privileges given to Cromberger, a building permit to Pablos allowing him to construct a house, the baptismal certificates for Pablos' son Alonso (1545) and daughter Elena, (1553), Pablos' statement of poverty to Viceroy Mendoza (1547), a loan to Pablos for purchasing printing equipment (1550), and other business records are cited or quoted by García Icazbalceta.[22] Pablos lost no time in getting to work to realize the pious objectives of Zumárraga. Unfortunately, there is no record of the present existence of the first American imprint of which we have undeniable evidence: *Breve y mas compendiosa doctrina christiana en lengua mexicana y castellana, que contiene las cosas mas necessarias de nuestra sanita fe catholica, para aprovechamiento destos indios naturales y salvacion de sus animas,* twelve quarto leaves with the imprint at the end: Mexico desta Nueva España, y a su costa, en casa de Juan Cromberger, año de mill y quinientos y treinta y nueve. We have this exact citation from the *Cartas de Indias* of 1867, and although García Icazbalceta made every possible effort to locate the copy from which the reference was taken, he was unsuccessful. There have been speculations as to the whereabouts of this precious quarto. Henry R. Wagner hazarded the guess that it belonged to José Sancho Rayón and passed from him to Fransisco Zabálburu, who owned part of the former's collection.[23] In *Excélsior* (Mexico) for 2 December 1944 Emilio Valtón wrote as though he had actually seen it: "Es in-4°, de 12 hojas, con tipos góticos de texto que miden unos 98 mm. en 20 lineas, de un cuerpo de algo más de 5 mm., equivalente a cerca 12 puntos modernos."

On 13 December 1540 Pablos issued a *Manual de Adultos,* a work of which only the two last leaves survive in the Biblioteca Nacional, Madrid. From the "fe de erratas" on the last folio it is clear that the book must have contained at least thirty-six leaves.

The recto of the first leaf contains Latin verse by Cristóbal **Cabrera**, who states that Vasco de Quiroga, bishop of Michuacán, ordered the printing of the *Manual de Adultos;* and this statement has been confirmed in a letter of 10 February 1567 by Pedro de Logroño, written in the Minas de Zacatecas: "Hize, yo el primero y no otro, el *Manual de Adultos para bautizar,* por orden y nota del obispo de Mechuacán." [24] In rather literal observance of the contract of 12 June 1539, the colophon states specifically that the book was printed "en casa d' Juá Cromberger."

The third known production of Pablos is the *Relación del espantable terremoto que agora nueuamente ha acontecido en la cibdad de Guatimala* (1541), four quarto leaves referring to the earthquake which wrought great destruction in Guatemala on 10-11 September 1541. [25] The fourth book known to have been printed in New Spain is a substantial work in eighty-four leaves, of which several good copies have survived: *Doctrina breve muy provechosa de las cosas que pertenecen a la fe catolica y a nuestra cristianidad en estilo llano para comun inteligencia* (1543). Several good copies have survived, and a complete reproduction, *The Doctrina breve in facsimile,* was published in 1928 as number 10 in the "Monograph Series" of the United States Catholic Historical Society.

Pablos' fourth book, the *Tripartito del Christianissimo y consolatorio doctor Juan Gerson* (1544) was translated from Latin into Spanish by Juan de Molina. Pablos' edition was reprinted page for page and almost line for line from the one printed by Remon de Petras in Toledo in 1526. In turn, Pablos' edition was reprinted in facsimile in 1949 in Mexico by the Ediciones "Libros de México" with a foreword by Alberto María Carreño. The importance of this work lies in the fact that it is the first known Mexican book with an illustration showing figures, an engraving on the verso of the title showing the Virgin investing Saint Alphonso with the chasuble. [26] The block from which the illustration was printed was most probably of Iberian origin.

In 1544 Pablos printed two editions of a *Compendio breve que tracta de la manera de como se han de hazer las processiones,* a small work in twelve and sixteen leaves (in the two editions, respectively) by the Carthusian Dionisio Richell (from Rickel near Liege), and the more important *Doctrina christiana para instrucion & informacion de los indios,* in thirty leaves, compiled by Pedro de Córdoba. [27] The significance of the latter work lies in the fact that for many years it was thought to be the first book printed in Mexico, hence the first American printed book. In 1545-46 Pablos printed the first part of another *Doctrina cristiana* which was in the Biblioteca Provincial of Toledo as late as 1863 but now known only through a lithographic facsimile of the title. It was once dated 1540, but García Icazbalceta presents evidence to disprove this ascription and that it was actually the first of another *Doctrina cristiana* of 1546 (his number 1). [28] A major tragedy is the apparent loss of a *Doctrina christiana breve traduzida en lengua Mexicana por el padre frai Alonso de Molina* (1546).

Pablos was looking forward by this time to the termination of his onerous contract with Cromberger, and his name first appears in a colophon as printer in the *Cancionero Spiritual* (1546), which has disappeared, but it does not appear in either the *Regla christiana* (1547) nor in the *Doctrina christiana en lengua Mexicana* (ca. 1547). For the first time in the *Doctrina christiana en lengua Española y Mexicana* (1548) we find the phrase "en Casa de Juan Pablos." From this time until his death in 1560 Pablos is known to have printed thirty-seven books during his active career, of which twenty-three came from his own firm from 1548 through 1560. His work achieved a relatively high standard of technical excellence, and it must have satisfied the ambitions of Zumárraga to bring a knowledge of Christian doctrine to New Spain. While the earliest imprints were religious in content, Pablos soon branched out into other fields such as law, science, medicine, and philosophy.

In 1548 Pablos issued the *Ordenancas y copilacion de leyes*, compiled by Viceroy Mendoza, the first legal code printed in the Americas. [29] There was no Latin edition of this work, contrary to the statement of Juan José de Eguiara y Eguren. [30] In 1554 Pablos brought Aristotle to the Americas with the *Dialectica resolutio cum textu Aristotelis* edited by the learned Augustinian Alonso de la Vera Cruz. [31] It may well be that the formal opening of the original University of Mexico, planned by Mendoza, on 25 January 1553 (although founded on 21 September 1551), had an effect on the subject matter represented in Pablos' lists. There were faculties of law, philosophy, and theology; and even though the university never enjoyed prestige comparable to that of later foundations in South America, notably, Córdoba, Lima (San Marcos), and Bogotá, it did receive much support from both church and state and exercised a strong influence on all aspects of Mexican culture including printing and publishing.

Pablos' support of scholarship may be seen in other imprints of the fifties. In 1556 he issued the first American arithmetic and algebra, the *Sumario compendioso de las quentas de plata y oro que en los reynos del Piru son necessarias a los mercadeyes: y todo genero de tratantes.* Con algunas reglas tocantes al *Arithmetica,* by an otherwise unknown friar named Juan Diez. Another monument of the history of science is Alonso de la Vera Cruz' *Phisica, Speculatio* (1557). Fray Alonso was one of the leading intellectual forces of his day, and he was appointed professor of scholastic theology when the university opened its doors in 1553. Although Pablos' publications in Mexican languages were in the service of propaganda of the faith--the original reason for the establishment of a press--Pablos' services to linguistic scholarship cannot be overlooked. In addition to the catechisms and other documents in the indigenous languages, Pablos also published several glossaries: Alonso de Molina's *Vocabulario en la lengua Castellana y Mexicana* (1553), Maturino Gilberti's *Arte de la lengua de Michuacan* (1558), and his *Vocabulario en lengua de Mechuacan* (1559).

Technically, Pablos' work leaves much to be desired. On the other hand, it compares favorably with that of other first presses in colonial jurisdictions. His use of type decorations and illustrations was not always judicious or appropriate, but he used what was available. He was economical in his use of wood engravings and did not discard them after a single use. In his edition of Alonso de la Vera Cruz's *Recognitio Summularum* (1554), Pablos introduced a wood engraving of Saint Augustine, which he used again in his *Constitutiones Fratrum Haerimitarum* (1556) [32] and bequeathed it with his other equipment to his successor and son-in-law, Pedro Ocharte, who used it in his *Doctrina christiana en lengua Guasteca.* A similar story may be told about an engraving of one of the most common of all sixteenth century

11

Mexican engravings, the stigmata of Saint Francis. Most curious of all is the *Dialectica resolutio* of Alonso de la Vera Cruz. The elaborate border with cherubs, warriors, a hippogryph, and a lion rampant-- *inter alia*--is virtually identical with that used by Edward Whitchurch in London for his *Booke of the Common Prayer*...(for Edward VI) in 1549. [33] Pablos even had some woodcut borders which he had dissected from originals and reassembled in fantastic combinations.

Perhaps Pablos' monopoly, which he enjoyed until the year before his death, made him a bit complacent. The monopoly was broken by the man whom Pablos himself brought to Mexico, Antonio de Espinosa. Espinosa was a man of considerable imagination and taste, and the books printed by Pablos in the fifties often reflect the competence of Espinosa. Up through 1553 Pablos printed with four sizes of a monotonous *rotunda.* The three Pablos imprints of 1554, Alonso de la Vera Cruz' *Recognitio summularum*, his *Dialectica resolutio*, and Francisco Cervantes de Salazar's *Dialogos* contain the first Roman and Italic types used in the New World. This was the work of Antonio Espinosa.

part ii

MEXICAN PRINTING FROM PABLOS' DEATH UNTIL THE END OF THE SIXTEENTH CENTURY

Antonio de Espinosa was the man who brought printing in Mexico to maturity. [34] He was one of four recruits brought to Mexico by Pablos to assist in a business which apparently began to prosper after Pablos gained full control. In 1550 Pablos sent an agent, Juan López, to Spain to purchase equipment ("aderezos") and to contract for assistants, above all, a craftsman who could cut and cast type. On 17 September 1550 López made a contract on behalf of Pablos with Tomé Rico ("tirador"--pressman) and Juan Muñoz ("componedor"--compositor) to work for Pablos for three years. [35] Much more important was the contract which López made on 24 September 1550 with Antonio de Espinosa, "fundidor de letra," to go to Mexico with his assistant, Diego de Montoya, and to work for Pablos for three years as "fundidor y cortador." [36]

The four new employees probably arrived in the spring of 1551. It is perhaps significant that nothing printed by Pablos in 1551 and 1552 survives, and it may be that he was waiting for the Roman and Italic types he began to use in 1554. In any event, the presence of Espinosa in Pablos' shop coincides with distinct improvements in typographical design and the use of ornamental pieces and engravings. There is no evidence to show how long Espinosa stayed in Mexico after he completed his three-year contract, but in 1558 at the court of Valladolid he represented himself as "avecindado en la Nueva España con su mujer y casa." He did stay long enough to become envious of Pablos' thriving business, and he was aware that the most recent of several renewals of Pablos' monopoly on printing in Mexico would expire in 1558. Accordingly he returned to the peninsula determined to secure permission to set up a press in competition with Pablos.

Espinosa's efforts at the court of Valladolid were successful, for on 7 September 1558 a royal *cédula* was issued stating that neither Juan Pablos ("ytaliano") nor anyone else might hinder Espinosa, Antonio Albarez, Sebastián Gutiérrez, and Juan Rodríguez, printers and legal residents of Mexico, from practicing the art of printing in their city. On 21 November 1558 Espinosa succeeded in getting two more *cédulas* directed to Viceroy Luis de Velasco directing him to assist Espinosa and to provide him with lots for building. [38] On 21 March 1559 Espinosa secured permission to return to New Spain and departed soon thereafter. On 2 and 3 August 1559 he presented the royal *cédulas* to Velasco with formal statements. [39]

His first imprint was the *Grammatica* of Maturin Gilberti, O.F.M., in Roman type and one of the best examples of Mexican presswork up to that time. His second work contained only twenty-six leaves of text, but it is one of his most noteworthy productions: Francisco Cervantes de Salazar, *Tumulo imperial de la gran ciudad de México* (1560). [40] The engraving of the imperial sepulcher of Charles V is quite remarkable for clarity and perspective, and García Icazbalceta argues that it must have been produced in Mexico, since the short period between the ceremonies and the printing of the book did not leave time for the engraving to be ordered from Spain. However, it is possible that the engraving was sent from Spain with the directive to print a memorial of the exequies.

Espinosa printed in Mexico until his death in 1576, with the exception of another three years he spent in Spain (1562-64). His most important typographical achievement came early in his career as an independent printer, the great *Missale romanum ordinarium* completed in September 1561. It is an impressive folio of 448 pages in two columns, in gothic type. The presswork is well-nigh perfect, with precise registration and inking, rare qualities in early Mexican books. Urgent business must have taken Espinosa back to Spain for the next three years, and Medina has speculated that the reason was to reinforce the directives in the two royal *cédulas*, which may not have been fully effective. [41] He resumed his printing in 1565 with a small work of twenty leaves, Alonso de Molina's *Confessionario breue, en lengua Mexicana y Castellana.*

In 1566 Espinosa printed another major work, Bartolomé de Ledesma's *De septem Novae legis sacramentis summarium,* a work of the same size as the *Missale romanum ordinarium,* but in Roman type, and with an architectural motif on the title page somewhat reminiscent of the *Tumulo imperial.* A significant work of 1568 is the *Graduale dominicale* of about 1568, which, unfortunately, survives only in a fragment in the Biblioteca Nacional in Mexico City. The imprint reads ''a costa de Pedro Ocharte,'' Pablos' son-in-law and successor, who had begun to issue books under his own name in 1563. Most likely the reason is that Espinosa, a skilled punch-cutter and type founder, had the better supply of types and music notes. Later, when Ocharte was incarcerated by the Holy Office in 1572, he asked Espinosa to print two

more books for him, a *Pasionero* and a *Graduale
dominicale,* but no copy of either survives. [42] Espinosa
continued his own printing until his death in 1576,
just after he had completed a *Graduale dominicale*
edited by Juan Hernández. This last work exists in
two states, one with a title page and colophon bearing
Espinosa's name (e.g., the copy in the Biblioteca
Nacional, Mexico), the other with a new title page
and colophon bearing the name of Pedro Ocharte.
Although the latter was probably locked out of his
printing house from 1572 to 1580, he was apparently
permitted to continue some of his activities as a publisher. Espinosa's business was inherited by his
young daughter María de Espinosa and rented to Peado
Balli (*infra*).

Espinosa was probably the best qualified printer
in sixteenth century Mexico, and his work provides
abundant evidence to support this assertion. Not only
were his design and presswork superior, but also his
use of engravings contrasts sharply with Pablos'
pedestrian ornamentation. A curious point which
emphasizes Espinosa's intimacy with the European
printers in the elaborate woodcut border on the title
page of the *Dialectica resolutio* (*supra*), bearing Pablos'
imprint but most probably designed and printed by
Espinosa. Incidentally, Espinosa was the only printer
of his day to use a pressmark.

According to the late Henry R. Wagner's calcu-
lations in his essay on "Sixteenth Century Mexican
Imprints" in the Wilberforce Eames festschrift, [43] 204
different Mexican books could be located in 1924. They
were produced by Pablos, Espinosa, and six other
printers (including one woman). Upon Pablos' death
(probably in 1560), his press passed to Pedro Ocharte
(or possibly Ochart, [44] according to Valtón, or Charté,

according to **Wagner** [45]), born in **Rouen** about 1532. It is likely that he arrived in Mexico around 1549, and he resided for a while in Zacatecas and Guadalajara as well as in the capital. Towards the end of 1561 or some time in 1562 he married María de Figueroa, daughter of Juan Pablos, by whom he had three children. He took over his father-in-law's business, and the first imprint that bears his name in a collection of *Prouisoes cedulas* dated 1563. [46]

Ocharte's career as a printer extended until 1592, when he produced Agustín Farfán's *Tractado brebe de medicina,* [47] the last title which bears his imprint. (This work should not be confused with Farfán's *Tractado breve de anothomia y chirvĝia,* printed by Antonio Ricardo in 1579). In all, Ocharte printed some thirty-five books, using an even richer variety of type (gothic, roman, italic) than Espinosa, for he combined what he inherited from Pablos with what he could purchase from Espinosa's type foundry. Moreover, he used a large number of woodcuts and rather elaborate initials. He printed a number of books in the indigenous languages of Mexico. One of Ocharte's most elaborate books is his *Psalterium, aniphonarium* [*sic*] *sanctorale, ou psalmis, & hymnis* (1584), described by García Icazbalceta, who owned the unique copy as a notable book executed with care and proves his point effectively with a facsimile of the title-page and one of f.89 ʳ. The *Antiphonarium* of 1589, of which the title-page was missing from García Icazbalceta's copy (now in the British Musuem; another copy in the New York Public Library), is a work of comparable quality. The so-called *Códice de Tlatelolco* [48] contains an autograph of Ocharte.

Apparently Ocharte's first wife, María de Figueroa, died some time in the latter part of the decade of the

1560s; and in 1570 he took a second wife, María de Sansoric, daughter of Pedro de Sansoric. We know that this second María presented him with a son, Pedro Ocharte, baptized on 17 June 1571. [49] She also supported her husband and his business valiantly when the hammer-blow fell from the minions of the Holy Office in 1572. This is an important point, since it was María de Sansoric, not the daughter of Juan Pablos, who used the imprint "apud viduam Petri Ocharte" on Manuel Alvarez' *De institutione grammatica libri tres* (1594).

It was possibly Ocharte's gallic *esprit* rather than any real heresy which attracted the critical attention of the Holy Office early in 1572, a tragic story which has been told in detail, with related inquisatorial activities, by Alberto María Carreño, along with other episodes involving the interest of this agency in allegedly heretical books found in the possession of printers, booksellers, and book collectors. The indictment (in Carreño's modern Spanish) states "que Pedro Ocharte, francés, impresor de libros, está anotado en los registros de esto Santo Oficio, haber acabado libros en que había opiniones luteranas contra la veneración e intercesión de los santos, afirmando que un solo dios se ha de rezar y no a ellos; y para confirmar lo primero, el propio Ocharte declara durante el proceso." [51] For six years Ocharte's business limped along, although he was apparently able to give it some supervision during the period when he was actually incarcerated. Thanks to the loyalty of María de Sansoric, who supervised the printing of "cartillas y los sumarios de Nuestra Señora del Rosario," and probably also to the sympathy of his competitor, Ocharte's business remained intact until he was again able to take over personally in 1578.

Ocharte was not the only printer to suffer from persecution by the Holy Office. One Juan Ortiz (also a Frenchman by birth, although brought up in Valladolid), an "imaginario," or manufacturer of *imágenes* (sacred pictures), was arrested at almost the same time as Ocharte. Ortiz was an artist of considerable ability, and his handsome engraving of the Virgin of the Rosary, 42 x 30 m., is preserved in the Archivo General de la Nación in Mexico City in the Inguisition file, Vol. LI, captioned "Proceso contra Joan Ortiz, ymaginario e Impresor natural del obispado de Gen en Francia vezino de Mexico." [53] The engraving is dated 1571 and was published by Ocharte, a fact which suggests that the Holy Office may have looked for guilt by association. The first accusation made against Ortiz was a condemnation of the viceroy and others for alleged mistreatment of Englishmen (probably merely an aspect of Spanish xenophobia during this period); but more serious was the charge of printing verses interpreted as heretical beneath the engraving, a quatrain of doggerel in small Gothic characters: "Estas cuentas so sin cuéta. En valor e yficacia. El peccador que os//reza, Jamas le faltara gra [i.e., gracis]." Ortiz' fate is uncertain, but he was found guilty, and Carreño hazards a fairly safe assumption that he fared worse than Ocharte.

A craftsman who was probably the fourth printer of New Spain was Antonio Alvarez (Albarez, *supra*), one of Espinosa's friends who joined him in the effort to break Pablos' monopoly. We know only that he was legally authorized to print and that he probably brought out a *Doctrina cristiana* in 1563, which, unfortunately, has not survived. [54] Thus the honor of being the fourth printer of Mexico must be given to Pedro Balli, probably a native of Salamanca although of ultimate French origin. [55]

Balli came to Mexico in 1569 as a bookseller, and in 1574, the first book with his imprint appeared: Juan Baptista de Lagunas, *Arte y dictionario: con otras obras, en lengua Michuacana.* The book is rather poorly printed and, indeed, Balli never distinguished himself as a typographer during the entire quarter of a century when he printed. It is likely that he started his career as a printer with rather modest equipment, since he seized the opportunity to rent Espinosa's shop and equipment immediately after the death of the latter in 1576. However, when Balli died in 1601, his heirs had to return Espinosa's types and press (or presses) to María de Espinosa, who had married a printer, Diego López Dávalos.

Balli printed more than sixty books during his active career. Many of his books were in the indigenous languages. There is, for example, the *Doctrina christiana muy cumplida...en léngua castellana y Mexicana* (1575), by Juan de la Anunciación, a typographically undistinguished work of 287 pages. The *Arte en lengua zapoteca* (1578), by Juan de Córdoba, is important mainly for notes on the calendar and Zapotecan antiquities. The *Arte en lengua Mixteca* (1593), by Antonio de los Reyes, has valuable notes on Mixtecan antiguities in the prologue. [56] The *Vocabulario en lengva misteca* (1593), by Francisco de Alvarado, is a significant bilingual glossary. Balli also had close association with the original University of Mexico, although it would not be correct to say that he had a university press even in the sense of contemporary Oxford. In 1596 he printed the *Oratio in lavdem ivrisprudentiae,* an academic lecture by his son, Juan Bautista Balli, an attorney of some distinction. Juan Bautista's memoir of his father is preserved in the Archivo de Indias. [57] Balli's last imprint Dionisio Ribera Flórez, *Relacion historiada de las exeqvias funerales de la magestad del rey D. Philippo II. Nuestro Señor. Hechas por el tribvnal del Sancto Officio de la Inquisicion desta Nueua España y sus prouincias, y yslas Philippinas* (1600). The full title is significant, for the work is a basic source on the history of the Holy Office in New Spain.

In 1608-1610 one Jerónimo Balli's name appears in the imprints of a few books and theses, and Medina [58] says it is "casi seguro" that he was the son of Pedro and the brother of Juan Bautista. From 1611 to 1613 Pedro Balli's widow, Catalina del Valle, operated the business, with one Cornelio Adriano César (whom Mr. Stols patriotically guesses was baptized Cornelis Adriaen de Keyser) as a compositor and pressman. [59] Subsequently the business was sold to María de Espinosa, by this time also the owner of the remnants of the equipment of Pedro Ocharte, inherited by his son, Melchor (*infra*). Thus there was an ultimate amalgamation of the shops and equipment (probably well worn and in poor shape) of Pablos, Ocharte (his successor), Balli, and Espinosa. The combined equipment was probably later sold to Diego Garrido (*infra*).

In some respects the fifth printer of New Spain, Antonio Ricardo (Ricciardi?), deserves the largest expression of gratitude of the Americas, for his great adventure in Peru (*infra*) must be added to his work in Mexico from 1577 to 1579. Ricardo was a Piedmontese from Turin. [60] A royal *cédula* of 1569 gave permission to Antonio Ricardo to emigrate to New Spain, [61] and he probably sailed at the earliest opportunity. He may have gone to New Spain as the result of some earlier association or correspondence with Espinosa or Ocharte. In any event, the imprint of Juan de Córdoba's *Vocabulario en lengua Çapoteca* (1578), reads, "Impresso, por Pedro Charte, y Antonio Ricardo." It is possible that some relative of Ricardo may have been printing in Spain, since Juan de Timoneda's *La primera parte de las patrañas* (Alcalá, Sebastian Martínez, 1576) has a notation dated 8 October 1576, "Alonso Ricardo, impresor." Again, it is possible that the Society of Jesus may have called Ricardo to New Spain, for in 1577 we find him with his own shop in the Jesuit Colegio de San Pedro y San Pablo in Mexico. The Jesuits had arrived in New Spain only in 1572, but it is likely that they began at once to give "special attention to the education of boys," a program for which a press was essential. From a typographical standpoint, Ricardo's work, both in Mexico and Lima, was above average, for example, his edition of Juan de la Anunciación's *Sermonario en lengua Mexicana* (1577), with other works. Some ten books printed by Ricardo, or associated with his name, reflect high standards of craftsmanship and editorial work. Ricardo left Mexico for Peru in 1580, and we will deal with his introduction of printing to the other American continent in a subsequent chapter.

The sixth printer in New Spain was Enrique Martínez, author, printer, punch-cutter, and engineer. His birthplace is located variously in Flanders, Andalucia, Hamburg, México itself, and France (the last vigorously supported by Medina [62]). From the sixteenth century there is but one imprint bearing his name, Elias de San Juan Bautista's *Compendio de las excelencias, de la bulla de la Sancta Cruzada, en lengua Mexicana* (1599). Medina was unequivocal in his opinion that Martínez was "El más notable de los impresores mexicanos del periodo que estudiamos," [63] although the historians' enthusiasm for Martínez' achievements are based more on his work as an engineer (for draining the Valley of Mexico in 1607) than for his monumental *Repertorio de los tiempos, y historia natvral desta Nveva Espana* (1606), a key document for the history of political, economic, and scientific achievements of Mexico in the sixteenth century. Martínez published several of his own works on various aspects of pure and applied science. He also printed books for the use of the Society of Jesus, among others a book described by García Icazbalceta as noteworthy for typographical excellence, *Poeticarum institutionum liber, variis ethnicorun, christianorumque exemplis illustratus, ad usum studiosae juventutis* (1605). [64] He printed for only twelve years, and the last book known to bear his name in the imprint appeared in 1611, the *Vocabulario* of Arenas. No other Mexican printer of the period, indeed few other contemporaries in any field, revealed comparable genius and versatility. Martínez died in Cuauhtitlán on Christmas Eve, 1632.

The seventh and last sixteenth century Mexican printer was Melchos (or Melchior) Ocharte, probably the son of Pedro Ocharte by his second marriage, born prior to 1574. In 1599 he printed the Franciscan Juan Bautista's *Confessionario en lengva mexicana y castellana*, one of the most extensive of all the Mexican *confesionarios* and a document which lends much to understand the customs of the Indians during this period. Another work printed by Ocharte for the same author is *Advertencias para los confessores de los Naturales* (1600-1601). The last record of Melchor Ocharte as a printer appears in the *Ramillete de flores divinas* (1605) of Bernardo de la Vega, of which he printed the first two fascicules and Diego López Dávalos the last. [65] Ocharte's shop was in the quarters of the Franciscan college in Tlaltelolco.

In Melchor's shop was one Luis Ocharte Figueroa, variously described as his brother (both being sons of María de Figueroa), his half brother (in which case Melchor would be the son of María de Sansoric), or even his nephew. Whatever the relationship, Luis completed the second part of Juan Bautista's *Advertencias* in 1601. M. Ocharte is on the title-page, but the colophon reads, "excudehat Lodouicus Ocharte Figueroa." Nothing is known for certain about Luis' other typographical activities.

The story of the book in the first century of the Spanish colonization of the Americas is still imperfectly known. The relationship of printers and booksellers is poorly known, although it is apparent that most printers also sold their own product. On the other hand, one **Andrés Martín**, who was not a printer, maintained a *tienda de libros* in Mexico, located in 1541 on the lower floor of a house in the complex of the Hospital del Amor de Dios. [66] A factor of some interest in that bookselling in the sixteenth century was not universally considered the honorable profession known today. In 1573 Viceroy Enríquez spoke of bookselling as being *en oficio bajo.* [67]

Thanks to the labors of devoted bibliographers such as Medina, García Icazbalceta, Millares Carlo, Valtón, Carreño, Wagner, and others, we know a good deal about Mexican "incunabula" (usually reserved for sixteenth century imprints). We are fortunate that so many copies of early Mexican books have actually survived. The elements--hurricanes, earthquakes, jungle humidity in the lowlands, and even volcanos-- have conspired against the survival of the sixteenth century Mexican book. The *polilla,* a papyrophilic insect with an enormous apetite, is un unrelenting enemy of all books between Miami and São Paulo. A chronic scarcity of paper, from Zumárraga's time onward, often discouraged book production in the colonial period. Censorship, a field which offers rich opportunity for study, was probably the reason that many a book was unwritten or unpublished. Then we must remember that most early Mexican books were printed with strictly practical objectives in mind, and a large proportion of surviving copies is grimy and dog-eared, often torn and lacking one or more pages. Some books have disappeared completely, a few without any positive evidence that they actually were printed.

The sixteenth-century Mexican printer produced utilitarian works needed in the daily work of the church, notably catechisms, prayer books, liturgical works, and, significantly, translations of practical religious works into the various languages of Mexico. There were also vocabularies and grammars of these languages. Law, medicine, physical science, and belletrictic letters were represented by relatively few titles. The clergy frowned on light reading, and no Mexican printer put out any *libros de cabellerias,* so beloved in Spain (but Mexicans were not denied of the privilege of reading these popular books). [68] There was a very substantial importation of scientific and scholarly books from Europe, a trend that has not changed after four and a half centuries. The sixteenth century Mexican printer did his best to satisfy the intellectual needs of New Spain; but his best was considerably less than what was needed, and it is likely that the number of books imported exceeded those printed locally in a large proportion.

part iii

PRINTING AFTER THE SIXTEENTH CENTURY IN MEXICO CITY

María de Espinosa's husband, Diego López Dávalos, printed with his father-in-law's equipment from 1601 to 1611. The acquisition of equipment of the Balli and Ocharte families has also been noted. López Dávalos completed Juan de Torquemada's *Vida de fray Sebastian de Aparicio* in 1602. The *Liber in quo quatuor passiones Christi Continentur* (1604) is a singularly well designed and printed book, and it is the last book printed in Gothic characters in Mexico and the only one in the seventeenth century. His last imprint was Martín de León's *Camino del cielo* (1611).

López Dávalos was indebted to the Holy Office for the services of Cornelio Adriano César, a skilled printer from Haarlem (*supra*). On 25 March 1601 the latter was sentenced to five years' imprisonment for Lutheranism, the first two to be spent in the Franciscan college in Tlatelolco, where Melchor Ocharte and López Dávalos operated. [69] (The printing activities of Ocharte and López Dávalos overlapped by a lustrum, but it is likely that neither could operate with regularity and that the Franciscans gave space to both in hope of having a regular printer.) César's name first appears in a fragment now in the Biblioteca Nacional, Mexico, entitled *Secunda para Calendarji ad usum Fratrum minorum pro anno Domini 1598* (1597): "TLATILULCO.   Ex Officina Vidue Petri Ocharte.   Apud Cornelium Adrianum Cesar." While César was being instructed in "nuestra santa fé católica y religión cristiana" in Tlatelolco, López Dávalos was able to use use his talents. His name appears in the life Sebastian de Aparicio as *cajista*. Nothing is known of his fate as a prisoner of the Inquisition, but in 1609 he re-appears as a compositor and pressman for Jeronimo Balli (the Ortografiá *castellana* of Mateo Alemán). His work with Pedro Balli's widow, Caterina del Valle, from 1611 to 1613 has already been noted. Caterina, who may have died in 1613, and he was with the shop of the "Herederos de Pedro Balli" well into 1614. When Diego Garrido acquired the old typographical equipment of Pablos, Ocharte, Balli, and Espinosa, it is possible that César joined him. In 1633 César, probably in his seventies, appears as a printer for Bernardo Calderón *(infra)*.

Diego Garrido's name first appears in 1615 as a tradesman "a la esquina de la calle de Tacuba," with no indication of his business, [70] but he was advertising two works printed by Juan Ruiz. In 1615 he is clearly established as a bookseller. Francisco Hernández' *Quatro libros de la naturaleza, y virtudes de las plantas, y animales que estan receuidos en el uso de medicina en la Nueva España* (1615) carries the following note in the imprint: "Véndense en la tienda de Diego Garrido, en la esquina de la calle de Tacuba, y en la Portería de S. Domingo." Garrido continued his work as printer and bookseller until 1625, the probable year of his death, and his widow ran the shop for at least two more years.

Juan Ruiz, whose books were sold by Garrido, first appears as a compositor in López Dávalos' office in 1612 and as an independent printer in the next year. Ruiz continued to print over the next six decades, and he enjoyed at one time the patronage of the Holy Office. His last work appeared in 1674, Burgoa's *Geográfica descripción*, and he died the following year. Among his other talents, he was also an astrologer. [71]

Early in 1617 Juan de Alcázar, or Juan Blanco de Alcázar began to print in Mexico City. He was perhaps the best educated of all early Mexican printers, a graduate of the University of Mexico, signing himself variously as "bachiller" or "licenciado." Typographically, his work was distinctly superior to that of his contemporaries. Especially impressive is his edition of Antonio del Pozo's *Monastica theologica* (1618). He also printed such important works as Martin de Léon's *Manual* (1617) and Diego Cisneros' *Sitio de México* (1618) with a portrait of the author engraved by Estradamus. The location of his shop in the Calle de Santo Domingo next door to the Inquisition might be a partial explanation for his privileges. The last work printed by Blanco de Alcázar in Mexico City appeared on Christmas Day, 1627. From that date until he reappeared as a printer in Puebla de los Angeles in 1646 (*infra*) we know nothing about his whereabouts or activities.

After Diego López Dávalos died, his widow carried on not only with César but also with Diego Garrido and Pedro Gutiérrez as compositors and probably also business managers. Pedro Gutiérrez also served Diego Garrido and his widow until 1628 (when the widow Garrido printed *El razonamiento del Marqués de Cerralbo* on 19 October of this year). Pedro Gutiérrez was also an independent printer in 1620-1621, beginning with Juan Coronel's *Discursos predicables* and concluding with Jerónimo Rubión's *Sermón* towards the end of 1621. Diego Gutiérrez, who was probably the son of Pedro, was also a compositor in Garrido's shop. In 1634 he printed Lorra Baquio's *Manual mexicano,* and his name continues to appear until 1643 when he moved to Puebla (*infra*).

The printers who were active in Mexico during the next century and a half until the immediate pre-revolutionary period can only be noted in broad outline, and we need urgently a revision of Medina with a commentary based on archives and records brought to light in recent years by Torre Revello, Leonadá and other contemporary scholars. We have such intriguing names in imprints as Pedro de Charte, who appears in the colophon of Jerônimo Moreno's *Relación breve,* two folio leaves bearing the date of 1630. There is strong reason to assume he was a close relative or son of Pedro Ocharte and had hispanicized his name, but proof positive is lacking. Bernardo Calderón, a native of Alcalá de Henares, [72] printed from 1631 to 1641 and was the founder of the most important family of printers in seventeenth-century Mexico. Calderón had such able employees as Pedro de Quiñones, who printed both independently and for others from 1631 until 1669, and Diego Gutiérrez, an able craftsman but restless. The latter may have acquired Garrido's vererable equipment, and he may have sold or turned it over for other considerations to Manuel de Olivos (or de los Olibos, as his name appears in two Puebla imprints of 1645). [73]

The Calderón family was one of the mainstays of printing in the last two centuries of Mexico's colonial period. Bernardo's widow, Doña Paula de Benavides, was an active and imaginative businesswoman and a fertile spouse, beginning with Antonio (born 1630), and including Gabriel, Diego, Bernardo, Maria and Micaela. She died at a venerable age in 1684 after having served the Mexican printing industry well for a half century. Among other commissions, the Holy Office used her facilities after its printer, Francisco Robledo (active as a printer from 1640 to 1647), died. Doña

Paula's children and heirs kept the business in the immediate family into the next century; and the names of Calderón and of associated families is found throughout the eighteenth century in Mexican imprints. The history of printing in eighteenth-century Mexico City, up to the period of independence is still a challenging field, and we need monographs on many of the individual printers in the light of subsequent research and new records of locations of copies presumed to be unknown, unique, or scarce three-quarters of a century ago.

NOTES

1. Joaquín García Icazbalceta, *Bibliografía mexicana del siglo XVI* (Mexico, Fondo de Cultura Económica, 1954; new ec. by Agustín Millares Carlo), pp. 23-24.

2. Seville, Archivo de Indias, Sección V. Audiencia de México, legajo 2555; cf. also José Toribio Medina, *La imprenta en México* (1529-1821) (Santiago de Chile, Impreso en casa del autor, 1908-1912; 8 vols.), I, xxxvi; García Icazbalceta, *Don fray Juan de Zumárraga, primer obispo y arzobispo de México; estudio biográfico y bibliográfico* (Mexico, Andrade y Morales, 1881), pp. 466-467; Emilio Valtón, *Impresos mexicanos del siglo XVI (incunables mexicanos) en la Biblioteca Nacional de México, el Museo Nacional y el Archivo General de la Nación; con cincuenta y dos láminas; estudio bibliográfico precedido de una introducción sobre los orígenes de la imprenta en América* (México, Imprenta universitaria, 1935), p. 6; and Mariano Cuevas, *Historia de la iglesia en México.* (El Paso, Texas, Editorial "Revista católica," 1928; 5 vols.), I, *apéndices,* pp. 46-47.

3. See the *cédula* real dated Talavera 6 June 1542, reprinted by García Icazbalceta, *Bibliografía mexicana del siglo XVI,* p. 45-46, and Medina, *op. cit.,* VIII, 384-385, from the original in the Archivo General de México, Libro II de Mercedes, ff. 48^V-49^r, actually ff. 46^V-47^r, expediente 120; cf. also Roman Zulaica Garate, *Los franciscanos y la imprenta en México en el siglo XVI; estudio bio-bibliográfico* (México, P. Robredo, 1939), pp. 285-287.

4. *Cartas de Indias* (Madrid, 1877), p. 786, col. 2; also in García Icazbalceta, *Don fray Juan de Zumárraga*, apéndice, no. 25.

5. Francisco Vindel, *El primer libro impreso en América fue para El rezo del Santo Rosario (Mejico, 1532-1534); facsimile estudios y comentarios* (Madrid, 1953), and *Apéndice* (Madrid, 1954).

6. Juan B. Iguiniz, Alberto Maria Carreño, and Federico Gómez Orozco, "Dictamen de la Academia Mexicana de la Historia Correspondiente de la Real de Madrid acerca del primer libro impreso en América según el señor Francisco Vindel," *Memorias de la Academia Mexicana de la Historia*, XIII (no. 1, January-March, 1954), 5-43.

7. Francisco Vindel, *Réplica en "Carta abierta" al dictamen emitido por la Academia Mexicana de la Historia* (Madrid, Imprenta Góngora, 1954).

8. Francisco Vindel, *En papel de Fabricación azteca fué impreso El primer libro en América (apuntes que comprueban la falta de veracidad en un dictamen de la Academia Mexicana de la Historia)* (Madrid, 1956).

9. Seville, Archivo de Indias; cited by García Icazbalceta, *Bibliografía mexicana del siglo XVI*, p. 42, and Medina, *op. cit.*, I, xlvii.

10. México, Archivo de la Ciudad, Libro IV de las Actas del Cabildo, 1536-1539, f.124^r; facsimile and transcription in Valtón, pl. 1 and p. 7.

11. Agustín Dávila Padilla, *Historia de la fundación y discurso de la Provincia de Santiago de México* (Madrid, 1596), p. 670; see also Manuel Sánchez Vale. "Está en Guanojato el primer libro impreso en América?," *Revista de Revistas,* XXV (no. 1317, 11 August 1935), [no page no.].

12. Alonso Fernández, *Historia Eclesiástica de nuestros tiempos* (Toledo, por la viuda de P. Rodriguez, 1611), p. 122.

13. Gil González Dávila, *Teatro eclesiástico de la primitiva iglesia de las Indias Occidentales* (Madrid, D. Diaz de la Carrera, 1649-1655; 2 vols.), I, 23.

14. Agustín Millares Carlo and Julián Calvo, *Juan Pablos, primero impresor que a esta tierra vino* (Mexico, Libreria de Manuel Porrúa, 1953).

15. This episode has been summarized by García Icazbalceta, *Bibliografía Mexicana del siglo XVI,* p. 25-26, from the sources.

16. *Ibid.,* p. 26.

17. The text has been printed *ibid.,* p. 42-44, from the original in the Archivo de Indias (Archivo Notarial, Protocolo de Alonso de la Baviera, Oficio I, Libro I de 1539, f.1069). A complete and clear facsimile is urgently needed. A comparison of García Icazbalceta's text with a rather poor photographic copy in the University of Kentucky Library indicates that it is an accurate transcription.

18. Mexico, Archivo de la Ciudad, Libro IV de las Actas del Cabildo, 1536-1539, f.195 v.

19. Archivo de Indias (Archivo Notarial, Protocolo de Alonso de la Barrero, Oficio I, Libro I de 1539, f.1069 (12 June 1539).

20. *Ibid.*, f.1072 (12 June 1539).

21. Cited by José Gestoso y Pérez, *Noticias inéditas de impressores sevillanos* (Seville, 1924), p. 68.

22. *Bibliografía mexicana del siglo XVI*, p. 45-48.

23. *Nueva bibliografía mexicana del siglo XVI* (Mexico, 1946), p. 61.

24. *Cartas de Indias*, p. 251. A note on Cabrera might normally be expected in José Mariano Beristáin de Souza, *Biblioteca hispanoamericana Septentrional* (México, 1816-1821; 3 vols.). See the article on Cabrera in Nicolás Antonio, *Biblioteca hispanica nova*, I, 238. See also Gallardo, *Ensayo de una biblioteca de libros raros*, II, col. 164 (no. 1519).

25. The same *relación* appeared in Madrid without imprint. García Icazbalceta, *Bibliografía mexicana del siglo XVI*, p. 62, says that José Sancho Rayón made a lithographic facsimile of a Spanish edition in four folios without date or imprint.

26. Lawrence S. Thompson, "Book Illustration in Colonial Spanish America," in *Book Illustration, Papers Presented at the Third Rare Book Con-*

ference of the *American Literary Association* (Berlin, Gebruder Mann Verlag, 1963), p. 22.

27. If the imprint assigned to *El rezo del Santo Rosario* is ever established conclusively, it will have to be recognized as the first illustrated book printed in the Americas. Reproduced in facsimile by the Universidad de Trujillo in 1945 as vol. xxxviii of the "Publicaciones de la Universidad de Santo Domingo."

28. *Bibliografía mexicana del siglo XVI*, pp. 70, 74-76.

29. Facsimile edition in the "Colección de incunables americanos," vol. V (Madrid, Ediciones Cultura Hispánica, 1945).

30. *Bibliotheca mexicana*, p. 221.

31. Facsimile edition in the "Colección de incunables americanos," vol. II (1945).

32. This book also contained the first music printed in Mexico.

33. Lucy Eugenia Osborne, "The Whitchurch Compartment in London and Mexico," *The Library*, 4th ser., VIII (1927), 303-311.

34. Alexandre A. M. Stols, *Antonio de Espinosa, el segundo, impresor mexicano* (Mexico, Biblioteca Nacional, Instituto Bibliográfico Mexicano, Universidad Nacional Autónoma de México, 1962; [Publicación] vol. VII).

35. Sevilla, Archivo de Protocolos, Libro del año
1550. Oficio XV, Libro II, Escribanía de Juan
Franco, fol. 240v. Printed in *Documentos americanos del Archivo de Protocolos de Sevilla, siglo
XVI* (Madrid, 1935).

36. Gestoso y Pérez, *op. cit.*, pp. 115-117, and Valtón,
op. cit., pp. 63-64.

37. Cited by García Icazbalceta, *Bibliografía mexicana
del siglo XVI*, p. 50, from the Archivo General de
la Nación (México), *Cedulario duplicado*, t.1, fols,
156r and v, expediente 148.

38. Cited *ibid*.

39. Cited *ibid*, pp. 50-51.

40. Facsimile edited by Justino Fernández and Edmundo
O'Gorman (Mexico, Alcancia, 1939).

41. *La imprenta en México (1539-1821)*.

42. Stols, *op. cit.*, p. 17.

43. Henry R. Wagner, "Sixteenth-Century Mexican
Imprints [and] Location Table of Mexican Sixteenth-Century Books," *Bibliographical Essays:
A Tribute to Wilberforce Eames*, 1924 reprinted
Freeport, N. Y., Books for Libraries Press, 1967,
pp. 249-268.

44. Emilio Valtón. "Pinceladas críticas. La *Nueva
Bibliografía mexicana del siglo XVI* del Dr. Henry
Wagner," *Excelsior* (México), 18 and 25 October,
1, 8, 15, and 29 November, and 6 December 1946,

no. 5 (15 October).

45. *Nueva bibliografía mexicana del siglo xvi*, p. 23.
The definitive work on Ocharte is Stols, *Pedro Ocharte, el tercer impresor mexicano* (Mexico, Imprenta Nuevo Mundo, 1962).

46. Facsimile in *Colección de incunables americanos*, vol. III (Madrid, Ediciones Cultura Hispánica, 1945).

47. *Facsimile in Colección de incunables Americanos*, vol. X (Madrid, Ediciones Cultura Hispánica, 1944).

48. Garcia Icazbalceta, *Bibliografía mexicana del siglo XVI*, p. 39, note 80, *et passim*.

49. México, Catedral, *Archivo de la Parroquia del Sagario*, Bautizos, Lib. III, f. 25r.

50. "La imprenta y la Inquisición en el siglo XVI," *Revista de revistas*, XV (1924), 19-21 (9 November 1924) and 38-40 (16 November 1924). Records of the Holy Office are fundamental of our knowledge of printing, bookselling, and book collecting in colonial Spanish America, since precise lists (not, however, in modern bibliographical form) were made of books seized incidental to arrest, *visita* reports of arriving bishops, and in related activities. See Irving Albert Leonard, *Books of the Brave; Being an Account of Books and of Men in the Spanish Conquest and Settlement of the Sixteenth-century New World* (Cambridge, Mass., Harvard University Press, 1949), and Lawrence S. Thompson, "The Libraries of Colonial Spanish America," in *Biblioteca docet; Festgabe ür Carl Wehmer* (Amster-

dam, Verlag der Erasmus-Buchhandlung, 1963), pp. 257-266.

51. Archivo General de la Nación (México), *Ramo Inquisición* (siglo XVI), t.51, no. 1.

52. Carreño, *op. cit.*

53. García Icazbalceta, *Bibliografía mexicana del siglo XVI*, no. 67 (p. 244); facsimile in Edmundo O'Gorman, "An Early Mexican Xylograph Incunable," *Mexican Art and Life*, no. 7, July, 1931, pp. 16-19; Lawrence C. Wroth, *Some Reflections on the Book Arts in Early Mexico* (Cambridge, Mass., Department of Printing and the Graphic Arts, Harvard College Library, 1945), p. [14-15].

54. García Icazbalceta, *Bibliografía mexicana del siglo XVI*, p. 36.

55. *Ibid.*, p. 37, note 66.

56. Pinelo-Barcia, *Epitome*, col. 725.

57. Sevilla, Archivo de Indias, 59-1-15.

58. *La imprenta en México* (1539-1821), I, p. cxx.

59. *Op. cit.*, p. 23-25; and logically, for he was a native of Haarlem (Archivo General de la Nación [México], Ramo Inquisición [siglo xvii], t. 788, f.270v).

60. So he himself says in Pedro de Oña, *Primera parte de Arauco domado* (Lima, 1596), and Miguel de Agia, *Parecer sobre la libertad de los indios*

(*ibid.*, 1604).

61. Sevilla, Archivo de Indias, 87-6-3, f.9 of the *Libro de cédulas reales.*

62. *La imprenta en México* (1539-1821), I, p. cx (suggests his real name was Henri Martin); the anonymous author of the article in the *Diccionario Porrúa de historia, biografía e geografía de México* (2d ed.; México, Editorial Porrúa, 1964), p. 955, thinks he was a Hamburger named Heinrich Martin.

63. *Ibid.;* the best work so far is Francisco de la Maza, *Enrico Martínez, cosmógrafo e impresor de España* (México, 1943).

64. Medina, *La imprenta en México* (1539-1821), II, 23-27 (no. 221).

65. García Icazbalceta, *Bibliografía mexicana del siglo xvi* p. 38, note 77, and references cited there.

66. Carreño, *Don Fray Juan de Zumárraga, teólogo y editor, humanista e inquisidor* (México, 1950), p. 145.

67. *Cartas de Indias,* p. 291.

68. Leonard, *Romances of Chivalry in the Spanish Indies with Some Registros of Shipments of Books to the Spanish Colonies* (Berkeley, 1933).

69. Archivo General de la Nación (México), *Ramo Inquisición* (siglo XVII), t. DCCLXXVIII, f.270v; Medina, *Historia del Tribunal del Santo Oficio de*

la Inquisición de México, p. 129.

70. Medina, *La imprenta en México* (1539-1821), I, cxxiii, with no source cited.

71. *Ibid.,* p. cxxii, citing Robles' *Diario.*

72. García Icazbalceta, *Obras,* IV, 65. Since the *Sermón* of Peralta Castañeda and the *Oración Funebre* of Rodriguez de León appeared in 1640, it seems likely that he may have lived at least until 1641, and that García Icazbalceta erroneously gives his death date as 1639.

73. José Toribio Medina, *La imprenta en la Puebla de los Angeles* (Santiago de Chile, Imprenta Cervantes, 1908), pp. 8-9; see also Stols, *op. cit.,* p. 24.

Chapter II

THE BEGINNING OF PRINTING IN PERU [1]

Antonio Ricardo [2] was not a failure in Mexico. During his active career as an independent printer in Mexico City, he produced ten books, or at least one every three months. Then he decided to move on to Peru, where in 1535 under Pizarro, Spanish soldiery had discovered and conquered riches that beggar the imagination. The new viceroyalty had thrived, and by 1551 it acquired the Universidad de San Marcos in Lima, oldest in the New World; but still there was no printing press. Ricardo may have been attracted either by the wealth of Peru or by the potential authors in the university, which was long to remain the intellectual capital of South America. A third possibility is that his patrons, the Jesuits, needed him in Lima. The first three Jesuits reached the viceroyalty of Peru in 1586, and others followed quickly on their heels. They may well have sent the word to the Colegio de San Pedro y San Pablo that a press in Lima (or La Ciudad de los Reyes, as it was first known and also appears in Ricardo's earliest imprints) would be of substantial help in realizing their aspirations to spiritual and temporal power.

Ricardo did not find it easy to move from Mexico to Peru. He was a foreigner, and as such he had to go to considerable trouble to get an entry permit for Peru. Ultimately, however, he was able to secure proper documentation and to book passage. He arrived in late 1580 or early 1581, but the first printed work from Lima that has survived is dated 1584. In any event, there is no evidence that Ricardo's services were not wanted, even though it might be difficult to get permission to establish a press. As early as 24 September 1572[3] the energetic Viceroy Francisco de Toledo wrote a letter (preserved in the Archivo de Indias) to the king urging that a catechism be translated into a composite Indian language, understood by all the people, and that it be printed either in Spain or in New Spain. Ten years later, on 30 September 1583, the Real Audiencia of Lima wrote a letter to the king (also in the Archivo de Indias) restating the need for a catechism in Quechua and Aymará, pointing out that "a well-equipped printer from Mexico is in our city" and urging His Majesty to issue this printer a license at once. However, before the king could act, the Audiencia took matters into its own hands on 13 February 1584 and granted Ricardo an exclusive license to print certain books under the supervision of the Jesuits and to sell them at strictly regulated prices. Ricardo was in business, and his license to print was confirmed by a royal cédula issued from San Lorenzo del Escorial later in the year.

Ricardo's first and most urgent task was to get a catechism in print, for the Audiencia's communication of 30 September 1583 had stated unequivocally that "any delay affects adversely the character of these Indians, as they lack knowledge of the Christian

Doctrine.'' The catechism was still not ready when
the summer mail from the metropolis arrived. It contained, *inter alia,* a directive from the Crown concerning the decision of Gregory XIII to reform the calendar.
Obviously, it was necessary to give widespread noti-
fication of this change, and Ricardo halted work on
his catechism to print a *Pragmatica sobre los diez
dias del ano,* signed by the Audiencia on 14 July
1584. This is the first product of the printing press
in South America, and the only surviving copies are
in the John Carter Brown Library of Providence, Rhode
Island and the Harvard University Library. 4

Work on the catechism must have been nearly
finished, for less than a month later, on 12 August
1584, the auto (certification) of the Audiencia was
affixed to the *Doctrina christiana y catecismo para
instrucción de los indios.* 5 (The rather absurd rumor
that a 1583 edition of this work was printed — without
any official permission whatsoever! — dies hard. The
copy in the Bartolomé Mitre Collection in Buenos
Aires has a torn title page on which the title and the
date 1583 are written in a crude hand, although the
imprint date of M.D.LXXXIIII, is clearly printed on
the part of the page that is preserved. There is a
facsimile of this title page in the *Gutenberg-Jahrbuch*
for 1931, p. 216). This book of ninety-two leaves
contains the Spanish text in a single column followed
by the Quechua and Aymará texts in parallel columns.
Besides being a monument of South American proto-
typography, this book also deserves recognition as a
hammer-blow by the Jesuits against a moribund heathen-
dom.

Ricardo printed two more books in 1585 for missionary purposes, a *Confesionario para los cvras de
Indios* 6 (possibly by Father Diego de Alcobaza, curate

of Capi in Cuzco and son of an early conquistador) and a *Tercero cathecismo*,[7] both in the same three languages as the *Doctrina christiana*. In 1586 came an *Arte, y vocabulario en la lengua general del Perv, llamada Ouichua, y en la lengua Espanola*,[8] attributed by Brunet and Medina to Father Domingo de Santo Tomás. We have no record of further activity by Ricardo until 1592 when he printed an *arancel real*.[9] In 1594 Ricardo printed a fifteen-leaf pamphlet by Pedro Balaguer de Salcedo [10] on the piracies of Sir Richard Hawkins, and the first vestige of a newspaper in the New World, a translation (on eight leaves) of a letter by "Ricardo Havqvines" to his father on his capture and the loss of his ship, *The Dainty*.[11] Medina records twelve sixteenth century imprints bearing Ricardo's name; and he describes twenty more in the next five years, ending with a *Sermón* [12] by Fray Pedro Gutiérrez Flores. In the next year (1606), so we learn from the *Libro de funerales de la Parroquía del Sagracio*, the mortal remains of Antonio Ricardo of Turin, "primer impressor en estos Reynos del Peru," were laid to rest in the Iglesia de Santo Domingo in Lima.

In 1605 appeared the first Lima imprint by Francisco del Canto Lozano, [13] Feliciano de Vega's *Relictio legis*, [14] a pamphlet in Latin in fifteen leaves. Canto, son of a printer in Medina del Campo, came to Lima in 1586, but we first learn of him as a printer in 1604 when the viceroy, Don Luis de Velasco, granted him a license to print. Canto introduced the refinement of two-color printing to Lima in 1608 with the *Directorio espiritval* [15] of Father Arriaga, and he was also a bookseller and probably the author an *Arte, y vocabulario en la lengua general del Perv, llamada Quichua, y en la lengua Española* [16] issued by his press in 1614. Although Canto was a fairly prolific printer, by the standards of his country and his age, he was probably not a good business man. He was imprisoned briefly for debt in 1617, and the next year he issued his last book, Antonio Rodríguez de León Pinelo's *Relacion de las fiestas que a la Immaculada Concepcion de la Virgen N. Señora se hizieron en la Real Ciudad de Lima.* [17]

There is a first-class mystery associated with Canto's name. In 1612 four books by Father Ludovico Bertonio appeared with imprints such as the following: "Impressa en la Casa de la Compania de Iesvs del pueblo de Iuli, que esta en la Provincia de Chycuyto, en la emprenta de Francisco del Canto, Ano M.DC.XII." [18] The four titles include a *Vocabvlario de la lengua aymara,* [19] a significant contribution to linguistics in some 900 pages, An *Arte de la lengva aymara,* [20] *Libro dela vida y milagros de Nvestro Senor Iesu Christo en dos lenguas, Aymara y Romance* [21] and a *Confessionario* [22] in Aymara and Spanish. One thing is certain: At some 12,000 feet above sea level a valiant band of Jesuits established a mission station and a college to facilitate the study of native languages at Julí on the Peruvian shore of Lake Titicaca. Between 1610 and 1612 a press, probably quite a different apparatus from the one producing books for Canto in Lima at the same time, was in operation in Julí. The Jesuits may have worked out some shadowy agreement with Canto whereby they could use his name, since he was a licensed printer, as a subterfuge to evade the vigilant zeal of the Audiencia in detecting unauthorized presses.

In 1613 the name of Pedro de Merchán Cálderon appeared in the imprint of a book printed in Lima, but seven years passed before another book appeared over his name and then only in three books printed in

1620. Merchán Calderón may have been associated with Canto during the seven years when nothing is heard of him.

In 1621 there appeared the first Lima imprint over the name of Jerónimo de Contreras, [24] progenitor of one of the most famous of all Latin American printing families. He opened a printing shop in Seville in 1618 and began to print some works of the learned Franciscan friar Alonso de Herrera, who had just arrived from Lima. Evidently the latter persuaded Contreras to emigrate to Peru, and there he had a productive and fruitful career until 1639. A slight but significant early publication by Contreras was a four-page new-sheet captioned *Nuevas de Castilla* [25] (1621). From then on such news-sheets containing resumés of the news brought by ship from Panama appeared fairly frequently, although the first American newspaper to be published periodically south of Mexico City was the *Gazeta de Lima,* which probably began publication in 1743. Native ability and a lucky marriage brought prosperity to Contreras, and in 1641 his son, José de Contreras, [26] took over the business and managed it for forty-seven years. Next in the line of succession was a grandson of the founder, José de Contreras y Alvarado, [27] Lima's only printer from 1688 to 1712. He secured the title of Royal Printer, and he was also printer to the Holy Office, the Tribunal of the Cruzada, and the Universidad de San Marcos. José's brother, Jerónimo de Contreras y Alvarado, [28] who had been printing since 1677, took over in 1712; and the last book to bear the Contreras imprint appeared in 1720. Even after 1720, however, the daughters of the family maintained an interest in the press, and it was actually operated by persons associated with the Contreras family until 1779.

The above-mentioned printers would appear to be the most important in Lima through the middle of the 18th century. It is true that Medina provides brief data on several dozen printers and presses through the end of the 18th century. However, many of these printed but a single volume and existed for a very short time.

The most important publishers of the last half of the 18th century are the Imprenta de la Calle de San Jacinto (1767-1784, 1820-1821), [29] Imprenta de los Huérfanos (1758-1824) [30] and Imprenta de Rio (1798-1824), [31] whose first publication was the *Telégrafo peruano.*

The Imprenta de los Ninos Huérfanos was the printer of colonial Spanish America's finest periodical, *Mercurio peruano de historia, literatura, y noticias públicas* [32] (12 volumes, 1791-1795) (a facsimile reproduction was published in Lima in 1964-1966).

Medina in his *La imprenta en Arequipa, El Cuzco, Trujillo y otros pueblos del Perú durante las companas de la independencia (1820-1825): notas bibliográficas* (Santiago de Chile, 1904; reprinted Amsterdam, N. Israel, 1964) notes that the first Arequipa imprint dates from 1821, that of El Cuzco from 1822, that of Trujillo from 1823. It is thus seen that Lima during the colonial period had a monopoly on printing in this area of the Spanish empire.

Medina finds several characteristics that are special to the typography of Lima. He notes that while it was customary in Spain, Mexico and Guatemala for the widows of printers to appear in imprints, this was never the case in Lima. He finds that the owners of printing establishments in Lima were often women who did not belong to the printers' guild. The only woman printer of Colonial Spanish America, Mónica

Sierra, was from Lima. [33]

For the whole colonial period Medina records
3,948 titles (including a few duplications) for Peru
and 12,412 for Mexico during the same period. Undoubtedly this proportion is characteristic of the relative
importance and wealth of the two viceroyalties. Nevertheless, in Latin America as well as Saxon America
we are constantly discovering colonial imprints both
at home and in such European depositories as the
Public Records Office and the Archivo de Indias.
There are discoveries to be made in the field of
colonial American typography that may be as spectacular as anything that could be revealed about the
mysteries of pre-Columbian history.

The content of Peruvian printing parallels that
of Mexico and other Spanish colonies, with strong
emphasis on religious texts (and particularly those
destined for mission purposes), law, some history,
some little science. Typographically the Lima imprints
are less distinguished than are those of Mexico and
Guatemala and even of some of the more remote South
American communities. The typical Peruvian book
was printed with poor ink of domestic manufacture,
worn types, unimaginative vignettes and decorative
pieces picked up second-hand in Spain and kept in
use for a century or more, and on creaky presses that
were refugees from the junk heap. Paper was scarce,
but Medina points out that nevertheless editions ran
into relatively high figures, from 500 to a thousand or
more. Still many of the more important Peruvian authors
sent their works to Spain or even to France and Germany to be printed. The colonial press of Latin America never was able to produce learned books in quantity,
and Peru is a noteworthy example of this disproportion
between the scholarly productivity of the friars and the

lawyers and the current status of printing technology.

NOTES

1. José Toribio Medina, *La imprenta en Lima (1584-1824)* (Santiago de Chile, 1904-1907; 4 vols.; reprinted in Amsterdam, N. Israel, 1965), is still the standard bibliography of early Peruvian imprints.

2. Medina, I, xix-xxxiii.

3. Medina, I, xxviii.

4. For a discussion and description of the copy of the *Pragmatica* in this library see, *Catalogue of the John Carter Brown Library in Brown University, Providence, Rhode Island*, N. Y., Kraus Reprint Corporation, 1961, 1:301.

5. Medina, I, 3-20.

6. Medina, I, 21-26.

7. Medina, I, 26-29.

8. Medina, I, 30-36.

9. Medina, I, 36-38.

10. Medina, I, 38-39.

11. Medina, I, 39.

12. Medina, I, 94.

13. Medina, xxxiv-xxxviii.

14. Medina, I, 94-95.

15. Medina, I, 108-109.

16. Medina, I, 133-135.

17. Medina, I, 150-151.

18. Medina, I, xxxviii-xl.

19. Medina, I, 118-120.

20. Medina, I, 120-124.

21. Medina, I, 124-126.

22. Medina, I, 126-130.

23. Medina, I, xl-xli.

24. Medina, I, xli-xliii.

25. Medina, I, 243.

26. Medina, II, 412-413.

27. Medina, I, xlix-l.

28. Medina, I, li.

29. Medina, I, lvii.

30. Medina, I, lvii-lxi.

31. Medina, I, lxiii-lxiv.

32. Medina, III, 220-226.

33. Medina, I, lxxxvi.

Chapter III

PRINTING IN THE REDUCCIONES OF
OLD PARAGUAY

When we speak of Paraguay [1] in the sixteenth and seventeenth centuries, we must remember that this term originally was applied not only to the country between the Paraguay and Paraná Rivers but also to adjacent parts of Brazil, Uruguay and of the Argentine provinces of Buenos Aires, Entre Rios, Corrientes, Missiones, and part of Santa Fé. Indeed, the actual site of the beginning of printing in old Paraguay was in the present Argentine territory of Missiones. In 1620 Paraguay proper and Río de la Plata (or Buenos Aires) were made separate jurisdictions, but both were dependent on Lima until 1776 when the viceroyalty of Buenos Aires was created with Paraguay as one of its dependencies. Franciscans and after them, Jesuits, had come to the Paraguay country in the decades after the founding of Asunción in 1535 by Juan de Ayolas, but it was only when a second band of Jesuits under Father José Cataldino, Simón Massetta, Marciel de Lorenzana and other leaders came to Paraguay in the first decade of the seventeenth century that the fan-

51

tastic Jesuit *imperium in imperio* of the *reducciones* (settlements of converted Indians) became a reality. Until their expulsion in 1767 the Jesuits worked with the Guaraníes intensively, and the results are truly remarkable, not least of all for the history of printing in the southern half of South America.

Elsewhere in Spanish America Indians were regarded as repartimientos or, later encomiendas, but the Jesuit fathers erected a curious sort of communistic-theocratic state in old Paraguay in which they, as spiritual and temporal overlords isolated their Indian wards from the corrupting influences of the Spanish colonial power. The Jesuit fathers taught the Indians trades and crafts, and the *reducciones* were all but self-supporting. Indeed, when printing finally came to old Paraguay, only the paper had to be imported from the old world.

Printing was an early desideratum for the *reducciones guaraníticas*. In the minutes of the fifth Paraguayan provincial conference of Jesuits held in Córdoba in 1633 the following urgent wish was expressed: ''Typographiam ad excudendam variorum Indicorum idiomatum, tum grammaticam, tum conciones pernecessarian enixe petit.''[2] The desire of the Jesuits was to use the printing press to publish works in the native language, something that they considered of the greatest necessity.

In this same year, an emissary of the Paraguyan fathers urged the Jesuit general, Mutio Vitelleschi, to send to Paraguay some brother from France, Flanders, or Germany who knew the art of printing. Despite repeated requests and even a directive from Vitelleschi to find a brother who could print, no practioner of the black art is known to have entered the Río de la Plata at this time. In their request to Vitelleschi, it was noted that grammars, dictionaries, catechisms and other works had been written in several of the Indian languages. It was decided not to try to have these works published in Europe because it was felt that they could not be printed without the assistance of those who understood these languages. [3]

Nevertheless, the fathers were determined to have books, and so books they had. They taught the Guaraníes to copy European books with such meticulous care that Father Francisco Zarque or Jarque remarked in his *Insignes misioneros* (Pamplona, 1687) that it was difficult to differentiate between a missal printed in Antwerp and the same book after it had been copied by the Indian scribes. [4] Various Spanish chroniclers of the period commented upon what they considered the special talents of the Guaraní in this area. [5] Book-length manuscripts exist which are of such high quality that one would take them for the work of the finest European printers.

Examples of these book-length manuscripts are Father Blas Pretorio's *Arte de la lengua guaraní* (1696) and Father Nicolás del Techo's *Decadas* preserved in Madrid's Archivo histórico. Thirty or more scribes are said to have worked on the copying of this volume.[6]

Even more interesting is the work which was done by the Guaraní xylographers. There is strong evidence on which to base a presumption that the Jesuit of old Paraguay had xylographic broadsides, pamphlets, or even books printed in the seventeenth century. A block found in Paraguay and presently owned by the Biblioteca Enrique Peña in Argentina is illustrated by a facsimile in Furlong's work. It is of the type that may have been cut by the Guaraníes, although it probably dates from the period subsequent to the expulsion of the Jesuits. [7]

Actual letterpress printing did not come to the La Plata basin before the beginning of the eighteenth century. The founders of the mission press were Father Juan Baptista Neumann (1659-1705) of Vienna and Father José Serrano of Antequera in Andalucia (1634-1713). These priests were the first to establish a printing press, to melt the necessary type and to produce the first Argentine books. Father Neumann arrived at the Río de la Plata in 1690. During his stay in the New World he won fame as an explorer. Serrano was head of the reducciones in the capacity of superior for a few months in 1695. He had a distinguished career as a teacher, scholar and missionary.[8]

The beginning of printing in old Paraguay is recorded by Father Antonio Sepp in his *Continuatio laborum apostolicorum ... in Paraquaria* (Ingolstadt, 1710) with a prologue dated 8 December 1701: "Hoc ipso anno [1700] J. Joannes Bapt. Neumann, ex Provincia Bohemiae, *Martyrologium Romanum,* quo hucusque plurimae Reductiones carebant, typis impressum, luci publicae exposuit, et licet impressioni Europae inaequales sunt litterae, sunt tamen legibles."[9] No copy of this first book, most likely printed in Loreto, in old Paraguay, has survived, nor has a copy of the 1709 (probably issued to correct many errors of the first), the fourth book printed in Paraguay; but we know of their existence from subsequent inventories of Jesuit libraries. We cannot be absolutely sure that the two *Martirologios* were in Guaraní, but it is likely that they were, or at least that they were bilingual.

Another basic document is a letter of 6 January 1696 from Tirso González, the Jesuit General in Rome, to Lauro Núñez, the provincial of Paraguay. González refers to translations into Guaraní of Pedro de Rivadeneira's *Flos Sanctorum,* and of Juan Eusebio

Nieremberg's *Diferencia entre lo temporal y eterno,*
being undertaken by Father Serrano; and, even more
significant, he expresses the desire that a press be
set up so that these books may be made accesible
to literate Indians. [10] Serrano completed the translation
of the *Flos Sanctorum* in 1699, [11] and on 18 September
1700 both this volume and the translation of the
Diferencia received the approval of the dean of the
Cathedral of Asunción.   No copy of the printed edition
of the *Flos Sanctorum* has survived, but we have a
record of its existence in Jesuit inventories compiled
before the expulsion.   Fortunately, we have two complete copies of the *Diferencia.*   It bears an unequivocal
imprint, "Impresa en las Doctrinas Ano de M.D.CC.V."
The actual place was most probably Loreto.   The
book contains 438 double-columned pages in small
folio, abundantly illustrated with woodcuts and decorative initials. [12]

All the valid evidence points to Father Neumann
as the creator of the press and types used in Paraguay.
The *Martirologio* [13] was probably a rather crude production, since it had to be revised in 1709; but Father
Serrano seems to have joined with the Austrian to
perfect the press and types in order to produce the
creditable *Diferencia.*   Certainly both of them were in
Loreto not later than the end of 1701, and it is un-
thinkable that the two should not have cooperated in
developing the new press in both technical and editorial matters.   Contrary to various speculations that
the types used at Loreto were cast from pure lead,
brass, or bronze, Furlong cites evidence that suggests
strongly that the type metal was a more or less con-
ventional alloy of lead and tin. [14]   In any event it
seems most likely that the type was cast in Paraguay.
Another unfounded allegation holds that the *Diferencia*

and possibly other early Paraguay imprints were produced clandestinely, despite the specific note on the
title-page of the *Diferencia* that it was produced "con
licencia del exelentissimo Senor D. Melcho Lasso de
la Vega Porto Carrera Virrey...del Perú." The
Jesuits did not have to print clandestinely, and, in fact,
the viceroy's written permission, dated 5 September
1703, exists today in Rio de Janeiro and is cited in
full by Furlong. [15]

The most fascinating possible relic of the press
of old Paraguay is a fragment of what Medina and
others allege to be the remains of the first press in
Loreto. The fragment so revered by Medina (probably
at the firm and patriotic insistence of General Mitre)
is now in the Museo del Cabildo in Buenos Aires,
where it has been fully reconstructed. The press
does undoubtedly date from a period prior to the nineteenth century, but neither Medina, Mitre nor any of
the historians who accepted their notions about the
old fragment have been able to cite any real evidence
that this press was used by the early printers of
Paraguay. [16] The first and essential material for printing, paper, was imported from Spain. It was the only
thing that the Jesuits did not produce, and, indeed,
they never succeeded in bringing a paper industry to
Río de la Plata country. [17]

Excluding spurious and doubtful titles, Furlong [18]
describes twenty-three Paraguay imprints issued during
the period from 1700-1727. Nine titles survive, and
of the other fourteen, nine are known only from Sepp's
Geschichte von Paraguai (1712; Munich, Staatsarchiv,
Hs. 275). We may grieve over all the lost titles, but
one in particular, Father Segismundo Aperger's *Tratado
breve de medicina* (1720), is a special tragedy, for
it was the first scientific treatise printed south of
Peru.

The imprints on the surviving titles indicate that printing was done in Loreto, Santa María la Mayor, San Javier, and possibly a fourth locality, which Furlong [19] suggests might be Candelaria, the see of the superior of the Jesuit missions in old Paraguay. All four places are located in the present Argentine federal territory of Misiones. There has been considerable debate as to whether there were several presses or one press moved from place to place. Various bibliographers have supported both views, and no real conclusion has been reached.

After 1727 we hear no more of the press of the Jesuit missions, and not until thirty-eight years later was there any printing anywhere in the La Plata basin, or at least none that is known at present. Various theories have been advanced to explain this abrupt end of one of the most fantastic printing ventures in history. There is evidence that the crown was not completely satisfied that printing by the Jesuits in the New World was a good thing. A likely explanation of the cessation of printing in Paraguay is that the uncomprehending Spanish colonial civil administrators disapproved of the use of indigenous dialects and tried to stamp them out. It was feared that continuing use of the native idiom was one of the strongest of all ties to freedom and independence, and we have substantial evidence of efforts to hispanicize the aborigenes. There is abundant evidence that no love was lost between viceregal authorities and the Jesuits, and the former placed many obstacles in the way of the latter. It is one of the curious facts of history that Anglo-Saxon Americans had no official obstacles placed in their way when they attempted to teach the Indians and publish in their language, but today Indian dialects in the United States have no importance as a linguistic element. Precisely the opposite is true in much of Spanish America and Luso-America.

NOTES

1. This chapter is based on the basic work of the late Guillermo Furlong, Cardiff, S. J., "La imprenta en las reducciones del Paraguay: 1700-1727," in *Historia y bibliografía de las primeras imprentas rioplatenses 1700-1850* (Buenos Aires, Editorial Guarania, 1953-1959; 3 vols.), I, 45-100.

2. Furlong, p. 46.

3. Furlong, p. 46.

4. Furlong, p. 50.

5. Furlong, pp. 50-52.

6. Furlong, p. 54.

7. Furlong, pp. 54-56.

8. Furlong, pp. 56-62.

9. Furlong, pp. 64, 309.

10. Furlong, pp. 64-66.

11. Furlong, pp. 65, 309, 311.

12. Furlong, pp. 68, 311-337.

13. Furlong, pp. 337-338.

14. Furlong, pp. 68-70.

15. Furlong, pp. 72-75.

16. Furlong, pp. 93-100.

17. Furlong, p. 72.

18. Furlong, pp. 309-417.

19. Furlong, pp. 75-78.

Chapter IV

THE BEGINNING OF PRINTING IN THE
RIO DE LA PLATA REGION

Today the great city of Buenos Aires and its hinterland are more important economically than any other region of Latin America, and it is somewhat astonishing to realize that printing did not come to the rich lands at the mouth of the Río de la Plata [1] until the latter part of the eighteenth century. The fact is that the population of Buenos Aires was relatively small (in 1770 there were slightly more than 20,000 people, of whom half were Negroes or civil and military officials), and for various reasons we cannot list in detail here, the cultural interests of the capital of the southernmost viceroyalty were relatively slight. Remote Chuquisaca (Sucre) or Guamanga (Ayacucho) had a more substantial cultural life than colonial Buenos Aires. [2]

Thus it was not in Buenos Aires but in Córdoba de Tucumán [3] where the first printing was done in Argentina. In that interior city, some 700 kilometers from Buenos Aires, the seventh university of colonial

Spanish America, the Jesuit Colegio Máximo de Córdoba, became the Universidad de San Ignacio in 1622 by papal and royal authority. The Jesuits, always indefatigable in their "peculiar care in the education of boys," found a home for their new university in the Convictorio de Montserrat and developed it into an important seat of learning.

It was not until November 1750, however, at the twenty-fourth Congregación Provincial, that the need for a press was expressed. Father Pedro de Arroyo and Father Carlos Gervasoni were elected to represent the Congregation at the courts of Rome and Madrid and to procure the necessary printing equipment. Unfortunately the star of the Jesuits was setting. Arroyo died in Madrid in 1753, and Gervasoni was expelled from Spain because of the vigor with which he defended the interests of the Indians in the matter of the Treaty of Limits.[4] Nevertheless, Gervasoni was able to buy a press, type, and other equipment in Italy and ship the whole to Córdoba in 1758 or soon thereafter.

A German Jesuit, Pablo Karrer,[5] a printer by profession, had been secured to operate the press as early as 1754. However, he stayed in Cadiz until 1764. Furlong suggests that he stayed this long in Cadiz because he knew that there was no press in Córdoba and that he wished to inspect the press before allowing it to be shipped to this city. The press and Karrer arrived in Córdoba the middle of July 1764. Furlong feels that it is possible and even probably that this press was installed by the end of August 1764. This press lasted for only two years, 1766 and 1767, the year of the expulsion of the Jesuits from all the Spanish dominions and the confiscation of their property.

Printing historians credit this press in Córdoba with five imprints. The first was *Clarisimi viri D. D.*

Ignatii Duartii et Quirosii Collegii Monserratensis Cordubae in America conditoris, laudationes quinque, quas eidem Collegio regio Barnabas Echaniquius... 1766. *Laudationes,* as it is usually referred to, is a collection of five speeches concerning Dr. Ignacio Duarte y Quirós, the university's greatest benefactor, by Father José Peramás.[6]

Five surviving copies are known. A facsimile with a Spanish translation was published in 1937 by the University of Córdoba's Instituto de estudios americanistas.

The other four imprints are all on religious topics. They are of the greatest rarity. Thus, *Instrucción pastoral del ilustrisimo Senor Arzobispo de París, sobre los atentados hechos a la authoridad de la Iglesia por los decretos de los Tribunales seculares en la causa de los Jesuítas* (1766) was known only through the unique copy in the Library of the Colegio de San Ignacio (Sarriá, Barcelona). This copy became lost, misplaced or destroyed as a result of the Spanish Civil War. [7]

The Franciscans occupied the Convictorio. On the orders of the Viceroy Juan José de Vértiz y Salcedo the press and the equipment were sent to Buenos Aires in 1780. [9]

From 1780, this Jesuit press was called "Imprenta de los Expósitos o de los niños expósitos" and was the only printing press in this part of America for a third of a century. [10]

José Torre Revello produced evidence in the *Boletín* of the *Instituto de Investigaciones históricas* (Buenos Aires) in 1943 that there may have been one or more small presses in Buenos Aires prior to the removal of the Jesuit press from Córdoba, but there is no evidence whatsoever to identify the printer or the shop. Until we can learn more about these presses, we cannot date the beginning of printing in Buenos Aires prior to 1780.[8]

Three men, Viceroy Vértiz,[11] a Portuguese bookseller named José Silva y Aguiar,[12] and Manuel Ignacio Fernández,[13] governor of the city, were largely responsible for the introduction of printing to Buenos Aires. As early as 1778 Vértiz wrote to the Franciscans in Córdoba inquiring about the press, now idle for nearly a dozen years. In 1779 Fernández had addressed a letter to the royal minister, José Gálvez, requesting a press for the community, largely for official purposes. He even attached a list of necessary type and a statement on the "modo de hacer tinta" (taken from contemporary texts) to his petition. It is probable that Silva y Aguiar was the source of these rather detailed specifications. Gálvez approved Fernández' request, but before Madrid could act, the energetic Vértiz had followed up his letter of 1778 to Córdoba, and early in 1780 the old Jesuit press with its equipment was in Buenos Aires.

A brief note concerning each of these individuals is perhaps pertinent.

Juan José de Vértiz y Salcedo was the viceroy from 1778 to 1784 and is considered one of the most progressive and enlightened in the colonial history of Spanish America; from 1770 to 1776 he was the governor of the area. His promotion to viceroy was received with much enthusiasm. Among the things done during his rule were the paving of the central streets of Buenos Aires, the reorganization of the orphans home, a correctional institution for women was established, and he worked for the establishment of a university.

Manuel Ignacio Fernández, the governor of Buenos Aires at this time, was a man of wide education. His library was an extraordinarily fine one and so great was his personal reputation that after he left his post no attempt was made to examine his stewardship, even though the Laws of the Indies prescribed such an examination for all crown officials. He died in Madrid in 1790.

Of the three, José Silva y Aguiar had the most knowledge of printing. He is referred to as a Portuguese. Vértiz placed the press under the jurisdiction of the Casa de Niños Expositos [14] (foundling home) which he established in 1779. The press would serve as a source of income for the Casa. Soon after the press arrived Silva y Aguiar offered to supervise its operation for the Niños Expositos, and Vértiz accepted his offer. The press was immediately put to work even without the customary royal approval.

In July 1779, Marcos José de Riglos, the prior sindico general of Buenos Aires, requested permission from the Viceroy José de Vértiz to establish La Casa de Niños Expositos (an orphan's home). The viceroy approved this petition by a decree of 14 July 1779 and steps were taken immediately to implement it. Funds were to be secured for the operation of the home from the profits of the printing press and a theater was also established in 1783, the proceeds of which were to assist the home.

Royal approval was given the establishment of a printing press in Buenos Aires by a royal cédula dated 13 September 1782. It is to be noted that printing began before this royal approval was received. One can only assume that the viceroy and his advisors must have felt that they were on reasonably safe grounds, for some 150 separate items had come off the press before royal approval was granted. [16]

Vértiz by a decree dated 21 November 1780 made

Silva y Aguiar the sole printer in the region for a period of ten years and he agreed that the government should assist in the establishment of the press in various ways. [17]

The press was first established on the corner of San José and San Francisco (now Peru and Moreno Streets). It stayed at this location from 1780 to 1783. From 1783 to 1824, it was on the corner of San José and San Carlos (now Peru and Alsina Streets). In both locations, the press was next to a book store behind the Colegio Grande de San Ignacio, then better known by its new title of Colegio Real de San Carlos. [18]

Silva was a bookseller and knew next to nothing of printing matters. He took charge of the press on 7 July 1780 and the next week Viceroy Vértiz wrote the governor of Montevideo to send to Buenos Aires Agustín Garrigós, a dragoon skillful in printing procedures. Garrigós was a native of Alicante (Valencia, Spain) and a printer by profession. He arrived in Buenos Aires on 2 August. He began immediately to work on the arrangement of the press and its equipment, which produced its first imprint in mid-October 1780. [19]

Garrigós served as the printer from August 1780 through mid-October 1791 having served under Silva y Aguiar, Sánchez Sotoca and Antonio José Dantás.

Two other soliders played important roles in the early days of the press. Antonio Ortiz, a native of Morón (Andalucia), began work at the press in September 1780 as a typesetter. It seems also that he may have owned a bookstore. Antonio López, a native of Ciudad Real (La Mancha), began work as a binder on 1 November 1780. Both were members of the Savoy Batallion. The press had the services for its first seven months of still another soldier, José Fernández. Several slaves and apprentices performed various tasks in the establishment. [20]

There has been discussion among historians of Buenos Aires imprints over what should be considered the first imprint from the Niños Expositos press. [21] Furlong presents data to show that J.M.J. / Letrilla, / Que llevaba / por registro en / Su Breviario la Serafica / Madre Santa Teresa de / Jesus. / Nada te turbe, nada / te espante; todo se pa- / sa; Dios no se muda; la / paciencia todo lo al- / canca: / Quien a Dios tiene / nada le falta; solo Dios basta. should be considered the press' first imprint. This religious poem was printed on one leaf and measured 140 x 222 millimeters. As of the early 1950's it existed in a unique copy in a private collection. [22]

Furlong provides such data and descriptions as can be produced on 235 imprints published between 1780 and 1784. The vast majority of these imprints were religious and governmental in nature and many are known only at second-hand as copies of many have not survived. [23]

From 1780 to 1783 Silva y Aguiar served as the head of the printing establishment as both the printer and the administrator. In 1783 serious accusations were made against Silva y Aguiar and the viceroy appointed Alfonso Sánchez Sotoca to be auditor. Sánchez Sotoca was to be assisted by Manuel Rodríguez de la Vega, Domingo Pérez and Francisco Basavilbaso. These four individuals found Silva y Aguiar impossible to deal with, for he feigned sickness or refused to provide them with the material that they required. The viceroy removed Silva y Aguiar from his position as printer and decreed the seizure of some of his property. He named Sánchez Sotoca to the post of printer.

Sánchez Sotoca was born in Parra (La Mancha). He was retired from the army on 28 November 1783 and died on 30 April 1791. He was the head of the printing establishment from 12 July 1783 to 15 July 1789. His administration was a highly honorable, loyal and correct one. The products of the press were not only greater in number and size, but the quality of the printing greatly improved. The printing establishment itself moved to more comodious quarters.[24] Silva y Aguiar did not take his removal kindly. He carried his case to the Audiencia, the highest court in the area, which decided that as long as the case was in litigation nothing new could take place in the administration of the printing establishment. This decision constituted a victory for Silva y Aguiar, for it meant that he legally remained in charge of the press although it was "de facto" under the control of Sánchez Sotoca. The suit lasted for six years. Matters were finally settled with Silva and his bondsman Antonio José Dantás now in control of the press, which they leased from the Hermandad de Caridad, the group that operated the Casa de Niños Expositos. Little is known of Dantás except from when he was a Portuguese businessman, who had moved to Buenos Aires with his family in 1777.[25]

Silva y Aguiar and Dantás fell out over business matters; suit was brought by Silva against Dantás; this was withdrawn and the matter brought to the governing body of the Hermandad de Caridad. The upshot of the affair was that Silva y Aguiar resigned from the printing establishment effective 20 December 1794. The running of the press was taken over by Dantás and his associate Francisco Antonio Marradas.[26]

Garrigós left the Niños Expositos in October 1791. He had expected to be appointed administrator of some village in Misiones. However, this project fell through and he desired to return to his position with the press. It was even his desire to replace Dantás in the leasing of the press. A conflict arose between the Hermandad de Caridad, which did not wish to re-employ Garrigós, and the new viceroy Pedro Melo de Portugal y Villena, who befriended Garrigós and insisted that he be returned to his former position. This conflict lasted from 1794 to 1796. [27] Melo forced Dantás to rehire Garrigós and at his former salary. The viceroy also gave Garrigós the title of master printer. [28]

When Dantás' lease expired in July 1799, Garrigós requested that the new viceroy, Antonio de Olaguer y Feliú, allow him to become the new leasor. He turned the request over to the governing body of the Hermandad de Caridad, which was forced to decide between the claims of Dantás and Garrigós. It finally decided in favor of Garrigós who took over the press on 17 October 1799 and was its head until 17 October 1804. [29]

The following individuals followed Garrigós as leasor of the Niños Expositos: Juan José Pérez, 1804-1809, [30] Agustín José Donado, [31] 1809-1812; José Rolland, [32] 1812-1816, Jaime Mora,[33] who died before even serving a full year. However, Mora was responsible for the acquisition of two new presses which were bought from an English merchant, Diego Brittain.

Besides printing works of various kinds, the Niños Expositos supplemented its income by binding, the production and sale of inks, the sale of paper at wholesale and by selling books brought from Spain.[34] By a decree of 1 December 1780, the viceroy granted the Niños Expositos a monopoly on the sale of readers, catechisms and primers for a period of ten years. [35]

Trisagio seráfico, para venerar e la muy Augusta y Santa Trinidad (1781) by Fray Eugenio de la San-

tísima Trinidad was the first volume to appear with
an engraving, the work of Juan Antonio Collejas y
Sandoval. [36] Among others who produced either copper
or wood engravings are: Pedro Carmona, Manuel Rivera,
Juan de Dios Rivera. [37]
The vast majority of the more than 2,000 works
published through 1810 dealt either with religious or
government matters, e.i., novenas, sermons, decrees
of the **viceroy** and other governing bodies. [38] Almost
nothing appeared that could be classified as belles-
lettres. Less than a dozen items, mostly in the field
of medicine, could be classified as dealing with the
sciences. Several imprints could be considered as
textbooks.

Two periodical ventures for this period are worthy
of mention: *Seminario de agricultura, industria y comercio* (1802-1807) [39] and the *Correo de comercio* (1810-
1811). [40] The first newspaper was the *Telegrafo
mercantil, rural, politico economico e historiografo del
Rio de la Plata* (1801-1802). [41]

Furlong found few cases of censorship either by
the state or the church. He mentions several cases
where civil or religious works were prevented from
appearing because they were considered either to
contain erroneous doctrine or because they were
dangerous. [42]

While this book is primarily designed to cover
printing in the colonial period, it would be improper
not to mention the first printing in a cultural center
as important as Montevideo [43] is today, especially in
view of the rather spectacular auspices under which
the art arrived in the Banda Oriental. Montevideo had
no press in the eighteenth century, and as late as
1807 it was only an overgrown provincial capital of
8,000 souls. [44] However, the rather sordid story of the

English efforts to invade the regions of the Río de
la Plata in 1806 and 1807 had a salubrious effect on
Uruguay in at least one respect. General Samuel
Auchmuty must have thought he came to found a new
empire, for the well equipped invasion fleet even had
a printing press (much as Napoleon's forces introduced
printing to Egypt with a shipboard press at Alexandria
and Cairo in 1798). Soon after Auchmuty assumed
control of Montevideo in February 1807, a weekly,
The Southern Star – La Estrella del Sur, [45] began to
appear; but it lasted only until 11 July 1807, after
General John Whitlocke's ignominious defeat and the
withdrawal of English forces from the Río de la Plata.
A facsimile was issued in 1942 by the Instituto Histórico y Geográfico del Uruguay under the editorship
of Ariosto D. González.

La *Estrella del Sur* had the following issues:
Prospectus (9 May 1807), first extra (10 May 1807, not
reproduced in the facsimile edition), seven numbers
(May 23, 30, June 6, 13, 20, 27, July 4, 1807), an
undated supplement and an extra dated July 11, 1807.
The press was located on Calle de San Diego, No. 4.
With the exception of the prospectus and the supplement, each issue contained four pages with four columns
to the page. [46] It was a bilingual newspaper. Some of
the material translated from English into Spanish was
extremely well done; the translation of certain other
items was both atrocious and unintelligible. [47] Scholars
apparently lean to the theory that William Scollay
(1785-1814) edited the paper under the direction of
the British military authorities. Scollay was born in
Boston and was a graduate of Harvard University. [48]

The paper published news which dealt with naval
matters as well as that which concerned foreign military
and political developments. Material was published

concerning the Río de la Plata area; there was an occasional literary piece. There were a variety of communications to the reader and each issue carried commerical advertising. [49]

When the newspaper ceased publication, the press and all of its equipment was moved to the Expósitos press in Buenos Aires. This was accomplished in early October 1807. [50]

Montevideo's second newspaper, *La Gazeta de Montevideo,* was established by the royalists in order to uphold the rights of Ferdinand VII and to counter the revolutionary tendencies of the *Gazeta de Buenos Aires.* [51]

The press was sent by the Infanta Carlota Joaquina from Rio de Janeiro in 1810, and it is the true cornerstone of printing in Uruguay. For this reason the Imprenta de la Ciudad de Montevideo was also popularly known as the Imprenta de Carlota. At least this one positive result may be traced to the unhappy rivalry between Argentina and Brazil for Uruguay in the two decades following the English invasion. [52]

The Prospectus (8 October 1810) and the first four numbers (13, 18, 25 and 30 October 1810) were edited by Nicolás Herrera. [53] From 6 November 1810-8 August 1811, it was edited by Mateo de la Portilla y Quadra [54] and from 8 August 1811 to 21 June 1814 Cirlo de Alameda y Brea. [55] Cirlo de Alameda y Brea later had a distinguished career as a clergyman. He was a general of the Franciscan order, archbishop of Santiago de Cuba, archbishop of Burgos and of Toledo and later a Cardinal.

The printing press which had been brought from Brazil was accompanied by two Portuguese typographers. Because of their ignorance of Spanish, the paper's first issue contained numerous typographical errors.

There was such a shortage of type that one had to compose and print one leaf at a time. [56]

After the Spanish were driven from Montevideo, the Imprenta de la Carlota continued in operation with the publication of *El Sol de las Provincias Unidas o Gazeta de Montevideo.* When troops from what is now Argentina evacuated Montevideo, they took with them this press. However, Artigas and the city council (cabildo) of Montevideo were able to abtain its return. In 1815 it began to publish *El Periódico Oriental.* This press lasted until 1819. [57]

NOTES

1. We follow the three volumes of Guillermo Furlong, *Historia y bibliografía de las primeras imprentas rioplatenses* 1700-1850. Vol. I (Buenos Aires, Editorial Guarania, 1953) has the following parts: La imprenta en las reducciones del Paraguay 1700-1727. La imprenta en Córdoba 1765-1767, and La imprenta en Buenos Aires 1780-1784. A history of printing is given for each of these areas followed by an extensive bibliography of imprints for the area and period covered. Vol. II (Buenos Aires, Librería del Plata, 1955) is La imprenta en Buenos Aires, 1785-1807. Vol. III (Buenos Aires, Librería del Plata, 1959) has two parts: La imprenta en Buenos Aires, 1808-1810 and La imprenta en Montevideo 1807-1810. As of 1975, these three extremely scholarly volumes, the work of a lifetime in the field, are all that have appeared. Furlong, vol. III, footnote 4, notes that Manuel Selva had promised to continue the bibliography from 1811 to 1850. Selva's death prevented the completion of the bibliography to this year. Furlong had in his possession many of Selva's bibliographical slips and hoped to be able to continue this bibliography. Whether Furlong's *Nochlass* is in a condition to be edited is not known.

   Furlong's three volumes have greatly added to the work done by José Toribio Medina, the great Chilean bibliographer, and numerous Argentine bibliographers.

2. Furlong, I, 115.

3. Furlong, I, 101-113, 419-452, III, 49-50.

4. Furlong, I, 102-105.

5. Furlong, I, 110-111.

6. Furlong, I, 419-436.

7. Furlong, I, 436-437.

8. Furlong, I, 118-125.

9. Furlong, I, 135-142.

10. Furlong, I, 130-135.

11. Furlong, I, 129-130.

12. Furlong, I, 145-150.

13. Furlong, I, 125-129.

14. Furlong, I, 130-135.

15. Furlong, I, 130-131.

16. Furlong, I, 150-152.

17. Furlong, I, 152-154.

18. Furlong, I, 154-158.

19. Furlong, I, 159-162.

20. Furlong, I, 162-167.

21. Furlong, I, 171-185.

22. Furlong, I, 453-457.

23. Furlong, I, 453-579 (nos. 1-235).

24. Furlong, I, 185-197.

25. Furlong, I, 197-202.

26. Furlong, I, 201-203.

27. Furlong, I, 203-209.

28. Furlong, I, 209-212.

29. Furlong, I, 212-214.

30. Furlong, I, 214-218.

31. Furlong, I, 218-219.

32. Furlong, I, 219-220.

33. Furlong, I, 220-221.

34. Furlong, I, 247-248.

35. Furlong, I, 240-247.

36. Furlong, I, 249.

37. Furlong, I, 248-260.

38. Furlong, especially I, 453-579 and Vols. II-III.

39. Furlong, II, 312-329, 373-383, 395-405, 420-429, 460-467, 558-561.

40. Furlong, III, 255-268.

41. Furlong, II, 262-299, 329-356.

42. Furlong, I, 263-266.

43. "La imprenta en Montevideo 1807-1810" in Furlong, *Historia y bibliografía de las primeras imprentas rioplatenses 1700-1850*, I, 275-303, is divided into two parts: I. La imprenta de *La Extrella del Sur*, pp. 275-291, and II. La imprenta de la ciudad de Montevideo (1810), pp. 292-303.

44. Furlong, I, 275.

45. Luis Alberto Musso, *"La Estrella del Sur"* (*"The Southern Star"*): *Indices analíticos para su estudio* (Montevideo, Florida Gadi, 1968), p. 5; Furlong, III, 391-402.

46. Furlong, I, 284.

47. Furlong, I, 284-285.

48. Furlong, I, 278-282.

49. See the index by Musso.

50. Furlong, I, 290-291.

51. Furlong, I, 292.

52. Furlong, I, 294.

53. Furlong, I, 300-301.

54. Furlong, I, 301.

55. Furlong, I, 301-304.

56. Furlong, I, 304-305.

57. Furlong, I, 305.

Chapter V

PRINTING IN PUEBLA AND CENTRAL AMERICA
IN THE SEVENTEENTH AND EIGHTEENTH
CENTURIES

The third place in which printing was established
in America, and, indeed, the fourth in the Americas
(after Mexico, Lima, and Cambridge) was the handsome
old city of Puebla de los Angeles.[1] So-called from the
pretty tradition that two angels added as much to the
walls of the magnificent Doric Cathedral (1552-1649)
as the workmen completed on the preceding day, Puebla
was founded in 1532, became an episcopal see in 1550),
and has always been recognized as the second city of
Mexico in cultural importance. The origins of printing
in Puebla are as obscure and controversial as they
are in Mexico City, and Medina has explored the problem fully in his *La imprenta en la Puebla de los
Angeles (1640-1821).*

The legend that a book was printed in Puebla in
1634 dies hard, and it still appears in **cheap** guide
books by chauvinistic *angelopolitanos.* Until 1943 the
first Puebla imprint was considered to be Father Mateo
Salcedo's *Arco triunfal: emblemas, geroglíficos y*

*poesías con que la ciudad de la Puebla recibio al
Virrey de Nueva España, Marques de Villena* [2] with
the simple imprint, "Impreso en la Puebla de los
Angeles, 1640." No Puebla imprints are known for
1641, but five titles appeared in 1643, viz., three
rather slight religious tracts without designation of
printer, and the humanitarian Bishop Juan de Palafox
y Mendoza's *Historia real sagrada* [3] (En la Ciudad de
los Angeles, por Francisco Robledo, Impresor del
Secreto del Santo Oficio, Año de 1643), and Bartolomé
Venavides y de la Cerda's *Sermon* [4] (En la Puebla de
los Angeles, por Diego Gutierrez, Año de 1643).

The authors are aware of the fact that Felipe
Teixidor in his *Adiciones a la Imprenta en la Puebla
de los Angeles de J. T. Medina* (pp. 3-4) argues that
the exact date of the *Arco triunfal* is not known and
therefore Teixidor would consider the first Puebla
imprint to be the *Svmario de las indvlgencias y per-
dones* published in 1642 by Pedro de Quiñones. Teixidor
would have Quiñones being a printer in Puebla from
1641-1643. This is the only Puebla imprint by this
printer recorded by Teixidor. This volume was first
described in 1943 by Salvador Ugarte in his *Notas de
bibliografía mexicana.*

Robledo's [5] name is the first to appear on a Puebla
imprint, but was he responsible for the *Arco triunfal?*
He started printing in Mexico City in 1640 and continued until 1647, when he probably died. He came
into contact with the bibliophilic Bishop Palafox in
1642, and in the same year he became printer in secret
to the Holy Office. It seems likely that Palafox
persuaded Robledo to send part of his equipment to
Puebla to print the *Historia real sagrada* and probably
also a *Carta pastoral* (one of the three 1643 Puebla
imprints without a printer's name). Robledo was

settled in Mexico before books appeared over his imprint in Puebla, and it is unlikely that he printed the *Arco triunfal,* unless (and this is improbable) he lived for a short while in Puebla before going to Mexico in 1640.

Medina suggests another possibility for the honor of being Puebla's first printer. The enigmatic Juan Blanco de Alcázar [6] printed some of the most typographically distinguished works of the seventeenth century in Mexico between 1617 and 1627 (notably Fray Antonio del Pozo's *Monastica theologica,* 1618). He disappeared completely for almost two decades, and suddenly, in 1646, his name reappears on a Puebla imprint. He was the printer of four rather slight works between 1646 and 1650. Blanco de Alcázar cannot be completely eliminated as Puebla's first printer. Medina finds no reason to attribute the *Arco triunfal* to Diego Gutiérrez, [7] whom we know to have been active as a printer in Mexico City from 1628 to 1634. Gutiérrez again appears in Mexico City in 1643 but he moved in that year to Puebla, printed the Venavides *Sermon,* and disappeared from typographical history.

The most important of all Puebla printers was Diego Fernández de León, [8] who practiced his craft in Puebla from 1683 to 1709. His establishment was a pretentious one, and in 1690 he had at least five assistants. In 1688 he received a large shipment of Dutch type from Spain, and from then on he called his shop the "Plantiniana." He was the first Puebla printer to use a device (a lion with a banner emblazoned with the initials DFDL), and his work was typographically attractive and textually significant. It is of some interest to note that the great printing firm of Calderón, which dominated publishing in Mexico City in the whole latter half of the seventeenth century,

also boasted of its Dutch type by applying to itself
the designations of "Plantin Press" and "Antwerp
Press."

By the eighteenth century printing was an established industry in Mexico City and Puebla, and the
growing wealth of colonial society provided an outlet
for an ever greater variety of books. Books on mining,
current events, history, geography and biography appear.
Strangely enough, printing did not come to Guadalajara,[9]
Puebla's rival for the rank of Mexico's second city,
until 1793. In the next year Veracruz [10] acquired a
press. A press was installed in Oaxaca in 1811, although almost one full century earlier there had been
another press in the southern metropolis. In 1720
Doña Francisca Flores issued Fray Sebastian de
Santander's *Sermon funebre* [12] on Mother Iacinta Maria
Anna of the Convent of St. Catherine of Siena, a
pamphlet of twelve leaves. There is no other extant
piece of printing from this press, and we know nothing
of what may have happened to the equipment. Doña
Francisca died in 1725, and we know only that she
made the Convent of St. Catherine her sole beneficiary.
When Oaxaca again acquired a printing house, it was
under the direction of a priest named José María
Idiaquez. In the midst of the revolutionary dis-
turbances of the day Idiaquez [13] was compelled to found
type, a feat that rivals the work of Antonio de Espinosa
and of the Jesuits of old Paraguay.

The third early center of printing in Spanish North
America and the fifth in the western hemisphere was
Guatemala, [14] and again here there has been some
uncertainty concerning the first Guatemalan imprint.
(It must be remembered that prior to 1779 Guatemala
in an imprint refers to what we now know as Antigua,
or Santiago de los Caballeros la Nueva, the beautiful

old city destroyed by the earthquake of 1773).

Though it would seem that Medina, in his classic *La Imprenta en Guatemala* (1660-1821) (1910) had demolished effectively the tradition that there was printing in Guatemala before 1660, there continued to be arguments concerning this matter as late as 1960. Alexandre A. M. Stols published in this year *La introducción de la imprenta en Guatemala.* In this volume Stols comments in detail on the arguments of of J. Antonio Villacorta C. who presented arguments to support the belief that the first Guatemalan book was *El puntero apuntado*... trabajado por un religioso del Orden de N.S.P.S. Francisco, de la Provincia de Guathemala. Con permisso de los Superiores. Año de 1641. Stols notes that the only surviving copy of this work is in the Medina library and that the date appears to have been retouched with ink. Stols points out that the date could have been misprint for 1741. He also collects most of the known data concerning Juan de Dios del Cid who died in 1746 to show that Dios del Cid, who is credited with being the author of *El puntero apuntado*, could not have written and published the volume in 1641. [15]

It was the distinguished Father Payo Enríquez de Ribera (1612-1685) who was responsible for bringing the black art to the land of the Quetzal. He was the son of Fernando Enríquez de Rivera, Duke of Alba and Alcalá, Viceroy of Naples, and of Leonor Marnique. He was educated at the Universities of Salamanca and Osuna. At the age of sixteen he became a member of the Agustinian order. He was bishop of Guatemala from 23 February 1659 to 3 February 1669. He was viceroy of New Spain from 1673 to 1681. [16]

Bishop Enríquez de Ribera commissioned Fray Francisco de Borja to go to Mexico where he was to buy a printing press and contract for the services of a printer who might wish to move to Guatemala.

Borja interested a Puebla printer, José de Pineda Ibarra (1629-1680) to establish himself in Guatemala. Pineda had worked in several printing establishments in Mexico City before moving to Puebla. Apparently he was not well-off as a printer in Puebla and he accepted with pleasure the contract offered him by Francisco de Borja.

He opened his print shop on 16 July 1660 in the city of Santiago de los Caballeros de Guatemala. [17]

According to the printer his press "was provided with everything necessary for its proper functioning and all the implements necessary for binding." The press itself cost 2,548 pesos and 6 reales. He was granted the exclusive privilege to print primers and catechisms by the Captain General don Martin Carlos de Mencos. [18]

In 1660 the new printer managed to produce three rather slight pieces of which we have a record. Medina accords the honor of number one in his list to Fray Francisco de Quiñones y Escobedo's *Sermon* preached on 4 October 1660. For 1661 we have no recorded Guatemalan imprint, but for 1663 we have two small pieces and Fray Payo de Ribera's monumental *Explicatio apologetica nonnullarum propositionum a theologo quodam non dextere notatarum*, a work of 710 pages on which Pineda Ibarra must have been working since his first arrival. [19]

The *Explicatio* and the Dominician Fr. Diego Saenz Ovecuri's *Thomasiada* (1667), an epic poem of genuine merit, are Pineda Ibarra's principal works. [20] He continued to print at a fairly steady pace until 1679. After Pineda Ibarra's death in 1680, his son, Antonio de Pineda Ibarra, who had been born in Guatemala in

1661, took over the press and operated it at the same leisurely pace from 1681 to 1721. He was the only printer in Guatemala until 1714. [21]

A second press was established in 1714 in the San Francisco Convent. According to its license, its purpose was to publish the *Crónica de la provincia del santisimo nombre de Jesus de Guatemala* by the Franciscan Fray Francisco Vasquez. This history was published in two volumes, 1714 and 1716. It is of interest that this set contained two metal plates engraved by Baltasar España. [22]

Antonio Velasco was a printer in Santiago de los Caballeros from 1715-1726. One of the outstanding works from his press was a reprint of Bishop Marroquin's *Doctrina cristiana en lengua guatemalteca* (1724). This publication used the special letters invented by Father Francisco de la Parra in order to represent phonemes peculiar to the Cakchiquel language. Velasco was the first to make use of these special characters and the first to show that he could reproduce any kind of needed type. [23]

Sebastian de Arévalo (1727-1772) became a printer at an early age. He too became apt at making his own type and in his publication of Fray Ildefonso Flores' *Arte de la lengua cakchiquel* (1753) he used the alphabet invented for this language by Francisco de la Parra. Medina claimed that his work ''constituted typographical specimens among the most interesting of their time in America'' including works illustrated with engravings by excellent artists. [24] Arévalo was also the publisher of Guatemala's first newspaper, the *Gaceta de Guatemala* (1729-1731). The *Gaceta* was the second Latin American newspaper to be published and appeared seven years after the *Gaceta de Mexico*. [25]

Cristóbal de Hincapié Meléndez (1689-1748) became a printer in 1739. He is better known for his work in botanical medicine. He printed chiefly novenas, theses and a few sermons. [26]

Joaquín de Arévalo, brother of Sebastian de Arévalo, was a printer from 1751-1775. From 1756 he served as the printer for the ecclesiastical tribunals. [27]

Antonio Sánchez Cubillas was a Spanish printer brought to Guatemala by Francisco de Vega, archdeacon of the Cathedral of Guatemala. Father Vega had bought a printing press in Spain for 17,000 pesos. Sánchez Cubillas served as a printer from 1772 to 1785. After the earthquake of 1773, he moved his press several times and in 1776 moved it to the new capital, Nueva Goatemala de la Asunción. In 1777 he became the government printer and later he was the printer of the ecclesiastic tribunals. [28]

His works are described by Vela as "magnificent examples of typography" and he had a large clientele. He decided to return to Spain and on 18 June 1785 he sold his press to Ignacio Quiroz y Beteta for 1,300 pesos. According to Medina, Sánchez Cubillas was the first to inaugurate the custom of numbering the pages of a printed work in Guatemala. [29]

Juana Martínez Batres, the widow of Sebastian de Arévalo, operated a printing establishment from 1775-1800. During this quarter century she bought three presses. The first was bought in 1775 the year in which the imprint "Viuda de Sebastian de Arevalo" first appeared in Paris for 850 pesos. Later she purchased a press in Spain for 2,000 pesos and still later another for 3,500 pesos. Her first publications were almanacs, novenas, catechisms and readers for children. [30]

Ignacio Beteta (1757-1827) became a printer in 1785 and was known for his interest in the graphic arts. He learned about printing from Sánchez Cubillas. He introduced many engravings in his publications and published the first *Guía de forasteros* under the auspices of President Bernardo Troncoso, who granted him a privilege for the publication of the *Guías*. He was the publisher of the *Gaceta de Guatemala*, 1793 or 1794- and 1797-1816. He was also the publisher of the newspapers that favored the independence movement, *El editor constitucional* and *El genio de la libertad*. On 15 September 1821 he renamed his printing establishment Imprenta de la libertad. [31]

Alejo Mariano Bracamonte y Lerin was a printer from 1789 to 1798. [32] Manuel José Arévalo who was a printer from 1803-1826 is apparently the last of the important colonial printers. [33]

Guatemala gained its independence in 1820 and its early political history was a troubled one.

The most important contribution of Guatemalan printers to typography was their use of the five special characters invented by Father Francisco de la Parra. Father de la Parra came to Guatemala before 1542 and produced a trilingual glossary in Quiche, Cakchiquel and Tzutuhil. The five special characters which represented sounds characteristic of the local languages stayed in use for three and one half **centuries.** [34]

The first printers in Guatemala produced volumes with illustrations and engravings. Among the more important engravers were Baltasar España and Pedro Garci-Aguirre, who taught generations of engravers, and whose pupils, according to Medina "carried the art of engraving in Guatemala to a splendor unknown in all the Spanish American colonies if we make an exception of Mexico. [35]

Printing was introduced into the other Central American countries, i.e., Costa Rica, El Salvador,

Nicaragua and Honduras after this area had gained its independence from Spain. Hence, printing in this area falls outside the interest of this discussion.

NOTES

1. The chief authorities for the study of printing in Puebla are: José Toribio Medina, *La imprenta en Puebla de los Angeles (1640-1821)* (Santiago de Chile, Imprenta Cervantes, 1908; reprinted Amsterdam, N. Israel, 1964) and Felipe Teixidor, *Adiciones a La imprenta en la Puebla de los Angeles de J. T. Medina* (Mexico, 1961).

2. Medina, pp. 3-4.

3. Medina, pp. 5-6.

4. Medina, p. 7.

5. Medina, p. xi-xiii.

6. Medina, pp. xiii-xv.

7. Medina, pp. xv-xvi.

8. Medina, pp. xvii-xxx.

9. José Toribio Medina, *La imprenta en Guadalajara de Mexico (1793-1821): notas bibliográficas* (Santiago de Chile, Imprenta Elzeviriana, 1904) would still seem to be the fullest discussion on the city.

10. José Toribio Medina, *La imprenta en Veracruz 1784-1821): notas bibliográficas* (Santiago de Chile, Imprenta Elzeviriana, 1904; reprinted in Amsterdam, N. Israel, 1964).

11. José Toribio Medina, *La imprenta en Oaxaca 1720-1820): notas bibliográficas* (Santiago de Chile, Imprenta Elzeviriana, 1904; reprinted in Amsterdam, N. Israel, 1964).

12. Medina, *La imprenta en Oaxaca*, pp. 11-12.

13. Medina, *La imprenta en Oaxaca*, pp. ix-x.

14. The chief sources for the early history of printing in Guatemala are: José Toribio Medina, *La imprenta en Guatemala (1660-1821)* (Santiago de Chile, Impreso en Casa Jilantor, 1910; reprinted Amsterdam, N. Israel, 1964); the late Alexander A. M. Stols, *La introducción de la imprenta en Guatemala* (Mexico, Universidad Nacional Autónoma de Mexico, 1960): David Vela, *La imprenta en la Guatemala colonial* (Guatemala, Editorial del Ministerio de Educación Pública, 1960); and Victor Miguel Díaz, *Historia de la imprenta en Guatemala desde los tiempos de la colonia, hasta la época actual* (Guatemala, Tipografía Nacional, 1930).
    The Vela volume cites no authorities except Medina and provides no bibliography of the subject. It reproduces in facsimile fourteen title pages.

15. The Stols volume has the following sections: Introducción, La imprenta no existió en Guatemala antes de 1660; La primera imprenta guatemalteca; José de Pineda Ibarra; primer impresor guate-

malteco; 1660-1679. The Appendix reproduces articles by J. Antonio Villacorta C. which were published in *El Imparcial*, 21 March, 26 April, 2 May 1956, A. A. M. Stols' reply to these articles in *El Imparcial* of 5 May 1956 and José Luis Reyes M.'s articles of 4 May 1956. These articles all deal with Juan de Dios del Cid and *El puntero apuntado*.

16. Vela, pp. 9-10.

17. Stols, pp. 20-24; Vela, p. 12.

18. Vela, p. 12-14, 18; Medina, pp. xvii-xx.

19. Vela, pp. 18, 20, 39; Medina, p. 6.

20. Vela, p. 39; Medina, pp. 14-17.

21. Vela, p. 20; Medina, pp. xxi-xxiii.

22. Vela, pp. 20, 23; Medina, pp. xxiii-xxv.

23. Vela, p. 25; Medina, pp. xxv-xxvi.

24. Vela, pp. 25-26; Medina, pp. xxvii-xxviii.

25. Vela, p. 26; Medina, pp. 74-77.

26. Vela, p. 27; Medina, pp. xxx-xxxiv.

27. Vela, p. 27; Medina, pp. xxxiv-xxxv.

28. Vela, pp. 27, 29; Medina, pp. xxxv-xxxviii.

29. Vela, p. 29; Medina, p. xxxviii.

30. Vela, pp. 29, 31; Medina, pp. xxxvii-xxxix.

31. Vela, pp. 31, 33; Medina, pp. xxxix-xlii.

32. Vela, p. 33; Medina, pp. xlii-xliv.

33. Vela, p. 33; Medina, pp. xliv-xlv.

34. Vela, pp. 33, 36.

35. Vela, pp. 37-38; Medina, pp. xlvi-liv.

Chapter VI

THE BEGINNING OF PRINTING IN
THE VICEROYALTY OF NEW GRANADA

In the eighteenth century the viceroyalty of Nueva Granada included the Presidency of Quito,[1] the Audiencia of Sante Fé (de Bogotá)[2] and the captaincy general and Presidency of Caracas.[3]

This jurisdiction held together until after the wars of liberation. The break-up was natural, since the area is far from homogeneous; but royal authority maintained it in the colonial period, and therefore its printing history may be considered here in a single chapter.

Again in this jurisdiction there are uncertainties and obscure references which may conceivably lead to concrete discoveries in the future. The redoubtable Gonzalo Jiménez de Quesada, en route to find El Dorado, founded Santa Fé de Bogotá in 1538, and there is some evidence that the Franciscans or their friends were printing there before the end of the century. In the July-September, 1957, issue of the *Revista interamericana de bibliografía* Juan Friede cites a document in the Archivo de Indias which indicates that the

Franciscan friar Pedro de Aguado sought permission to go to Nueva Granada to supervise the printing of his *Historia del Nuevo Reino de Granada,* since no books had been printed there before. On 5 February 1582 permission was granted, but the story ends here in a complete blank. [4]

The first printing of which we have definite evidence in Bogotá is dated exactly two centuries after the foundation of the city. The Jesuits were responsible for the founding of the press, and here the first Bogotá imprint of which we have any record is Father Juan Ricaurte y Terreros, *Septenario al corazón doloroso de María Santissima,* with the imprint "Con licencia. En Santa Fé de Bogotá: En la Imprenta de la Compania de Jesus. Año de 1738." [5]

The Jesuit Father Antonio Naya was granted permission by the Royal Audiencia on 10 December 1737, to establish a press which was to publish books of Catholic doctrine and devotional works. Brother Francisco de la Peña (1716-?) was the first printer to become established in what is now the Colombian capital. He was born in Madrid and joined the Jesuit order in 1734 and reached New Granada in 1735. [6]

In his *Bibliografía bogotana* (1917) Eduardo Posada identifies ten imprints (one not located but known to have been printed) from this Jesuit press between 1738 and 1742. The press served religious purposes exclusively, for eight of its nine surviving imprints are *septenarios, novenas* or similar publications, while the other deals with the privileges of the Jesuits. [7]

This Jesuit press continued in operation through 1767, the year in which the Jesuits were expelled from all Spanish territories. [8]

The second city of what is now Colombia to have a printing press was Cartegena de Indias. Joseph de Rioja established a press in this city in 1769 and published in this year Marcos Antonio de Ribera's *Novena del glorioso mártir San Sebastián patrón contra la peste.* Unfortunately almost nothing is known concerning the fate of this press as this is the only known imprint from Cartagena for 1769-1773. [8] In 1774, Antonio Espinosa de los Monteros established a printing press in Cartagena and its first publication was Francisco Antón Vélez Ladrón de Guevara's *Octavario que a la Inmaculada Concepcion*... [9] In 1777 Espinosa de los Monteros moved his press to Bogotá at the suggestion of the viceroy Manuel Antonio Flórez. [10] The first imprints from this press whose owner acquired what was left of the old establishment of the Jesuit fathers were issued in 1778 and many of the publications bear the imprint"... Imprenta Real de D. Antonio Espinosa de los Monteros." [11]

From 1738-1784 the Colombian imprints could be classified as novenas, works of religious piety, broadsides and a few official documents. In 1785 there appeared several forerunners of Colombian journalism. *Aviso del terremoto* was printed by Espinosa de los Monteros and had three issues in 1785. To this day no one knows anything of the editors of the *Aviso*. [12] The same printer in the same year issued the *Gazeta de Santa fé de Bogotá Capital del Nuevo Reyno de Granada.* Three numbers of this 4-page journal have survived. They are dated Aug. 31, Sept. 30 and Oct. 31, 1785. [13] It is thought that the *Gazeta* was edited by the same group of individuals who edited the *Aviso*.

Cauca Prada consider the first book to be published in Colombia to be Josef Luis Asula y Lozano's *Historia de Christo Paciente* which was published in 1787. Cauca Prada apparently bases his definition of the word book as a work of a certain length. This particular work was in two volumes and contained a total of 494 pages. [14]

The most important newspaper of the late 1790's was *Papel periódico de la Ciudad de Santafé de Bogotá* which began publication on Feb. 9, 1791. It had 265 numbers and ceased publication on Jan. 6, 1797. It did not appear from Oct. 5, 1792, to April 19, 1793 It was directed by Manuel del Socorro Rodríguez and among its contributors were many of the Colombian intellectuals of the period. [15]

In 1791, Antonio Nariño acquired a printing press which began to function under the direction of Diego Espinosa de loa Monteros in March, 1793. Antonio Nariño is considered by many to be one of the precursors of the Colombian independence movement. He is known also as the translator from the French of *Derechos del hombre y del ciudadano* (1794). He was tried for his part in its translation and publication and sentenced to exile. [16]

The Imprenta Real continued under Antonio Espinosa until 1804, when his son Bruno took it over. Once again, in 1810 "La Patriótica" appears as the name of a printing shop under Nicolás Calvo. New presses came in from the United States, and printing throve mightily in Colombia during the revolutionary decade.

The period immediately preceding Colombian independence saw the appearance of numerous political and government newspapers, many of which were short-lived. The Spanish authorities of the period did not approve of the use of printing or of its spreading. In short, the leaders of the independence movement made ample use of the printing press as a vehicle for the expression and publication of their ideas. [17]

Printing in Ecuador is another chapter in the triumphs and tragedies of the Company of Jesus in

Latin America. As early as 1736-1740 the Jesuits
tried to get a license to print from the Real Audencia
in Quito, but they had no success. In 1740 two prominent Ecuadorean Jesuits, José Maugeri, a Sicilian
by birth, and Tomas Nieto Polo del Aguila, a native
of Popayán (Colombia) were sent to Europe with
various objectives, one of which was to buy a press
for the private use of their community. With them was
one Alejandro Coronado, a poor copyist of Quito who
worked for the Jesuit residence. It would appear that
the two priests arranged for Coronado to secure a
royal cédula from the Consejo de Indias, permitting
him to operate a public printing office in Quito. Coronado, a man of humble circumstances, could not buy
a press, but the Jesuits could; and their equipment,
with Coronado's license, could permit the establishment
of a public press. Coronado died in Spain, and his
mother, Angela, in Quito inherited the rights granted
by the cédula. The Jesuits then arranged for her to
sign over the cédula to Raimundo de Salazar. In the
meantime, however, the press which the fathers bought
or intended to buy did not reach Ecuador, and Salazar
could do nothing. Sra. Angela Coronado revoked the
earlier contract and turned over the cédula to the
procurador of the Colegio Maximo of the Jesuits. [18]

When and how a press reached Ecuador we do not
know. When it did, it was established in the new
Jesuit college in Ambato, some seventy-five miles
south of Quito. We do not know the exact reasons
why it was located there. We may guess that it was
at the instigation of Father Maugeri, who was probably
the moving spirit behind the importation of the press
and who founded the college at great personal sacri-
fice. The first printer was Juan Adán Schwartz,
probably a native of Hamburg, who entered the Jesuit
order in 1751 and arrived in Quito in 1754. Schwartz'

first production came in 1755, St. Bonaventure's *Piisima erga Dei genetricem devotio*, a substantial publication of ninety-two pages. In the next four years, until 1759, eleven other books and pamphlets, all of less than a hundred pages, appeared in Ambato.

It is to be noted that these Ambato imprints were all works which dealt with religion. Four of these works are anonymous; two are by St. Buenaventura, while others are by José Maríz Maugeri (?), Juan de Velasco (?), Pedro José Milanesio, Juan Bautista Aguirre, Buenaventura Suarez and Pope Clement VIII and Pope Urban VIII.

From the technical and aesthetic point of view, the books and broadsides printed by Schwartz show good taste and typographical knowledge. The style of his title-pages and of the composition of his pages greatly influenced Raimundo Salazar. The typographical material, bought in 1754, more or less, was of the school of the great master Claude Garamond (16th century) and established the stylistic pattern of the Ecuadorean books of the colonial period. [19]

In 1759 Father Maugeri and the printing press moved from Ambato to Quito. Fifteen Quito imprints are known to exist printed between 1759 and 1767, the date of the expulsion of the Jesuit order from Ecuador. A sixteenth imprint was printed either in Ambato or Quito.

These publications were the work for the most part of Schwartz; an anonymous imprint may have been the work of the printer Raimundo de Salazar, who from 1757 had been the owner of a small press. [20]

In 1767 the Jesuit printing press came under the control of the Spanish king; members of the order were expelled from the New World, the order's property confiscated. Juan Adán Schwartz, Ecuador's first printer, died on November 26, 1767, in the Gulf of Darien.[21]

Raimundo de Salazar's first known imprint, *Novena al glorioso San Nicolás el Magno* was published in Quito in 1762. It is still not known when Salazar obtained a printing license, bought his press in Lima and became established as a printer. His only imprints were devout pamphlets, invoices, etc. for he had not yet been granted a royal cédula which would authorize him to print books.

Little is known of Ecuadorean imprints for the period 1767-1779. Salazar produced three religious works during this period and apparently was allowed to use the confiscated Jesuit press.

In 1779, according to Gonzáles Suárez, the Jesuit printing press and equipment was handed over to Salazar. Salazar between 1779 and 1793, the last date that his name appears on a title page, published slightly more than 55 books. During this period he served without pay as a kind of official printer as he printed the government documents of the time. Besides official and religious publications, he also printed a *Plan de estudios para la Real universidad de Santo Tomás.* [22]

José Mauricio de los Reyes published seven imprints from 1794 to 1799. In 1801 and 1802, Miguel de los Reyes published two imprints. Three of these nine items were only one leaf in length. [23]

From 1803 to 1816, there would appear to have been no imprints whatsoever printed, for no printed book has survived from this period.

Salazar was the printer of the first Ecuadorean newspaper, *Primicias de la cultura de Quito*, which was written by Dr. Francisco Javier Eugenio de Santa Cruz y Espejo. The issues of this journal appeared on Jan. 5, 19, Feb. 2, 16, March 1, 15 and 29, 1792.[24]

From 1816-1830, the following printers existed in Quito: Ignacio Vinuesa, Casa de Manuel de la Peña (up to 1825); Imprenta de Francisco Xavier de la Cruz (1816-1843 [?]), Imprenta del Gobierno (1823-1826); Imprenta de los Cuatro amigos del país (1826-1828), Imprenta de la Universidad central del Ecuador (1828-   ) and Imprenta de Gobierno Regente (1820-   ). [25]

The majority of the publications for the period 1816-1818 were broadsides or pamphlets of a more or less official character and are the work of Francisco Javier de la Cruz. He became the director of the "Imprenta del Gobierno" in 1823. New type was secured for this press of Didot or Bodoni style. [26]

Numerous newspapers were published in Quito; most of these were either issued by the government such as *Gaceta de Quito* (1829-1830) or were the organ for various religious or political factions. Thus, *El Imparcial del Ecuador* (1827-1828) was a pro-Bolívar, anti-Peruvian and federalist paper. All of them had a short life. [27]

The first printing press was brought to Guayaquil in 1821. [28] Manuel Ignacio Murillo was the first publisher in this city and the city's first imprint was *El patriota de Guayaquil*, whose first number is dated May 21, 1821. Most of the early imprints from this city are broadsides, patriotic songs, bulletins, proclamations, decrees and pamphlets concerning the area's incorporation into Peru. Almost no imprints for 1823-1825 have survived and because of the great fires of February 12, October 5, and 6, 1896, it is doubtful if the full bibliography of early Guayaquil imprints will ever be known. The period saw the publication of a number of short-lived newspapers. Of interest to students of literature was the appearance of José Joaquín de Olmedo's poem, *La victoria de Junín.*

Canto a Bolívar (Guayaquil, 1825). [29]

Printing was introduced to the city of Cuenca in 1828. Its first imprint was *El eco del Asuay,* a newspaper of which 26 numbers are said to have appeared. This newspaper was edited by Fray Vicente Solano. Other short-lived newspapers also edited by Solano appeared in the 1828-1830 period. Few other imprints from this period have survived and only a handful are known to exist. [30]

There has been much scholarly discussion concerning the first publication in what is now Venezuela. The argument has been over whether a volume by José Luis de Cisneros entitled *Descripción exacta de la provincia de Benezuela,* Valencia, 1764, was published in Valencia, the capital of the Venezuelean state of Carabobo. Pedro Grases has presented the fullest recent account of the scholarship on both sides of the question and has reached the conclusion that this volume was written early in 1764 and that it was dedicated to José Solano y Bote, governor and captain general of Venezuela. His research reveals that it was published in San Sebastián (Spain) on the official printing press of the Real Compañía Guipuzcoana de Caracas. Grases notes the extreme rarity of the volume; however, he points out that in recent years several copies have been discovered in San Sebastián which strengthens his view that this particular volume was printed in this city. [31]

It is of interest that the island of Trinidad was part of the political jurisdiction of the Captain generalcy of Venezuela until the Treaty of Amiens of 1802. This island was seized by the British in February 1797. Printing was introduced in Trinidad in 1789 and a *Gaceta* began publication in this same year. [32]

In the early part of the first decade of the nine-

teenth century there were references to printing presses that could be moved from city to city. Alexander von Humboldt claimed that Caracas had a printing press in 1806 and he credited Louis Delpech with being its founder. [33]

Francisco de Miranda (1750-1816), a precursor in the movement for the independence from Spain of its colonies, acquired a printing press from New York in January 1806 and it with six printers was placed on the "Leander". It is known for sure that between February 21 and March 27, 1806, this press published two documents and probably published two others. In August, three other documents were probably printed. They were printed in Jacmel so that Miranda could communicate with his fellow patriots on the mainland. This press was saved in the skirmish of Ocumare, but those who operated it were made prisoners. It continued its traveling in the Carribean Sea to Puerto España where a new group of printers put it again into operation. It operated out of the island of Aruba and after the failure of Miranda's plans, this press was acquired by Matthew Gallagher. [34]

Documents exist which show that in 1790 the Colegio de Abogados de Caracas desired to establish a printing press in Caracas and that in 1800, the Real Consulado de Caracas petitioned the Spanish crown for the establishment of a printing press. These two attempts both met in failure. [35]

Printing was introduced into Caracas in 1808 for policital reasons by the colonial authorities. It is noted that the *Gazeta de Caracas* (October 24, 1808-April, 1810) devoted almost all of its pages to political questions. It was this journal's purpose to orient public opinion, to counter tendentious doctrines and to publish whether from official or private sources whatever favorable news it received concerning the cause of the legitimate sovereigns.

Contemporaries of the press recognized its vital importance. Thus Fray Juan Antonio de Navarrete wrote in his manuscript preserved in the Biblioteca nacional, Arca de letras y teatro universal that in 1808 "there was established printing so desired in this city of Caracas". The first editorial of the *Gazeta de Caracas* which was probably written by Andrés Bello noted that a printing press had not existed in Caracas and it spoke of the fact that Caracas had envied smaller cities because they had a printing press.

In September, 1808, Francisco González de Linares conducted negotiations through Manuel Sorzano with Mateo Gallagher and Diego Lamb of Trinidad which resulted in the two printers establishing a printing press in Caracas. González de Linares was acting on behalf of Juan de Casas, captain general of Venezuela, and Juan Vicente de Arce, the intendant of the army. On September 12, 1808, Sorzano noted that the two printers were on the American frigate "Fénix" and were bound for the port of La Guaira. On the ship, the printers brought with them their clothing, a printing press and equipment necessary for the press. The great desire of the Caracas authorities for a printing press can be seen in the fact that all of the red-tape for its establishment had been cut in slightly more than a month. The press had been shipped from La Guaira, installed and begun to function; all formal documents had been taken care of within a period of 31 days.

The Imprenta Gallagher y Lamb was the only printing establishment in Caracas until Oct. 1810. Besides the publication of the *Gazeta de Caracas*, this firm between 1808 and 1812 printed a good handful of various types of publications: broadsides, pamphlets of sermons, almanacs, political documents of various kinds as well as a two-volume set of *Derechos de la América del Sur y México* by William Burke. [36]

The *Gazeta de Caracas* began publication on October 24, 1808, and issued its last number on January 3, 1822. From October 1812 to the early months of 1813 it was a Royalist organ; from August 1813 to June 1814, it was that of the government of Bolívar; it was once again a royalist organ until the battle of Carabobo in June, 1821, except for a few numbers published by General Bermúdez in May, 1821; from July, 1821, to January, 1822, it was a patriotic newspaper, organ of the Republic of Colombia.

The *Gazeta* had a series of editors. Its first was the famous Andrés Bello, who probably was its editor from October, 1808, until April 19, 1810, perhaps even until June, 1810.

Juan Baillío (1752-..) has been called by Pedro Grases the printer of the Independence movement. He established his press in Caracas in 1810 and issued on November 4, 1810, the first number of *Semanario de Caracas*. His press published broadsides, pamphlets, newspapers and books in 1810, 1811, 1812, 1813, 1814 and 1816.

He printed the *Semanario de Caracas, El Mercurio venezolano, El Patriota de Venezuela* and *El Publicisita de Venezuela,* newspapers. In 1813-1814 he is at Bolívar's side and has the title of "Printer of the Government".

Among the books which came from his press are: *Derechos del hombre y del Ciudadano;* **Condillac's** *Lógica o los primeros elementos del arte de pensar, Constitución federal para los Estados de Venezuela* and the *Contitución de la Provincia de Caracas.* [37]

Cumaná is the second Venezuelan city to have a printing press. Pedro Grases shows that this city's first publication, a *Manifiesto,* appeared on May 4, 1810. [38]

Ballío established a printing press in Valencia

in February, 1812. This press apparently printed little through mid-1812. From it, there appeared chiefly proclamations, *bandos* and a newspaper, *Boletín* of war. [39]

Notes

1. For printing in Ecuador our chief source has been Alexandre A. M. Stols, *Historia de la imprenta en el Ecuador 1755-1830*, Quito, Casa de la cultura ecuatoriana, 1953. Pages 163-166 provide a bibliography on studies of Ecuadorean printing. Part Seven, pp. 167-261 is a descriptive bibliography of Ecuadorean imprints for the period. Pp. 263-310 are reproductions of title pages.

2. The most recent discussion of the early history of printing in Colombia would seem to be Antonio Cauca Prada, *Historia del periodismo colombiano*, Bogotá, 1968. This is primarily a history of Colombian newspapers and periodicals. Pp. 381-388 are a bibliography of Colombian printing and of studies on Colombian journalism.

3. For Venezuela we have relied on Pedro Grases, *Historia de la imprenta en Venezuela hasta el fin de la primera república (1812)*, Caracas, Ediciones de la presidencia de la Republica, 1967. Pp. 229-233 are a bibliography of Venezuelan printing for this period. The volume contains 112 plates which reproduce title pages of books and pamphlets and early issues of journals and periodicals. Also of great value is Agustin Millares Carlo, *La imprenta y el periodismo en Venezuela desde sus orígenes hasta mediados del siglo xix*, [Caracas]. Monte Avila, [1969].

4. Cauca Prada, pp. 31-32.

5. Cauca Prada, pp. 25-26.

6. Cauca Prada, p. 24.

7. Eduardo Posada, *Bibliografía bogotana*, Bogotá, Imprenta de Arboleda y Valencia, 1917 (Biblioteca de historia nacional, 16-17), I, 1-25.

8. Cauca Prada, p. 34.

9. Cauca Prada, pp. 35-37.

10. Cauca Prada, p. 40.

11. Cauca Prada, p. 44.

12. Cauca Prada, p. 49.

13. Cauca Prada, p. 50.

14. Cauca Prada, p. 51.

15. Cauca Prada, pp. 55-58.

16. Cauca Prada, pp. 58-62.

17. Cauca Prada, pp. 63-94.

18. Stols, pp. 15-39.

19. Stols, pp. 43-50.

20. Stols, pp. 51-55.

21. Stols, pp. 56-58.

22. Stols, pp. 61-69.

23. Stols, pp. 73-74.

24. Stols, pp. 70-72.

25. Stols, p. 105.

26. Stols, pp. 98-99.

27. Stols, pp. 97-105.

28. Stols, pp. 106-112.

29. Stols, pp. 113-123.

30. Stols, pp. 124-134.

31. Grases, pp. 15-38.

32. Grases, pp. 41-43.

33. Grases, pp. 45-47.

34. Grases, pp. 49-67.

35. Grases, pp. 71-75.

36. Grases, pp. 79-119.

37. Grases, pp. 123-146.

38. Grases, pp. 149-151.

39. Grases, p. 155.

Chapter VII

THE BEGINNING OF PRINTING IN CHILE [1]

The origin of printing in Chile was long clouded in mystery, and even Medina was unaware of the real facts when he compiled *La imprenta en Santiago* (1891). Today it is generally accepted that the first press was brought to Chile by an aristocratic German Jesuit, Carlos Haimhausen. [2] According to Domingo Amunategui Solar's [3] account of the beginnings of printing in Chile, Father Haimhausen was sent to Spain as the *procurador* for the provincial congregation of Chile. He organized a missionary team of some forty individuals, many of them skilled artisans; and, what is more important, he acquired large stocks of supplies and equipment to promote trade and industry in Chile, up to that time primarily a colony of farmers and frontier fighters. When Haimhausen arrived in Buenos Aires in November 1747, he had his shipments checked by the officers of the captain-general of Buenos Aires, Don José de Adonaegui. The records show that the customs agents in Buenos Aires found "cinco cajones para imprenta de libros" among Haimhausen's 386 boxes and bundles; and we also know that royal officials in Santiago checked in these five boxes on 6 May 1748.

106

Most of Haimhausen's group was settled on the hacienda of Clarea de Tango with their equipment, but the press and the type were sent to the Universidad de San Felipe. It is not known whether it was used for printing prior to Haimhausen's death in May 1767 and the Jesuit expulsion four months later. At least nothing from this period of the press has been discovered.

The first surviving Chilean imprint that has come down to us is the *Modo de ganar el jubileo santo* (1776), a slender pamphlet of nine pages, extremely poorly printed. An unsatisfactory facsimile was published in 1910 by Ramón A. Laval under the title of *Un incunable chileno*. It was taken from the one surviving copy bound in a pamphlet volume once in the collection of Ramón Briseño and now in the Biblioteca nacional in Santiago. This copy is in bad condition and this factor, combined with the poor halftones, make the facsimile illegible in many places. [4] We know nothing about the printer or the conditions of printing, but there is no evidence that there was any press in Chile in 1776 other than the one imported by Father Haimhausen a quarter of a century earlier.

Medina records twenty-one pieces, mainly broadsides of an official character, printed in Santiago between 1780 and 1811 (in 1964, Feliú Cruz recorded 36 imprints for 1776-1811), [5] but in spite of Laval's discovery his assertion that Chile had no proper press during the colonial period is essentially correct. Chilean writers were compelled to send their manuscripts of books to the peninsula to be published. The noted Bishop Gaspar de Villaroel entrusted to a certain person some manuscripts and a substantial sum from his poor box for printing costs. The manuscripts were lost, and the agent embezzled the funds. Such was the problem that many a creative writer in Chile and, indeed in other places throughout the Indies, faced when he aspired to break into print.

It seems most likely that the Santiago imprints recorded by Medina were printed on Haimhausen's press, but only fragmentary information is available about the printers and the circumstances of printing. We know that there was a press (probably Haimhausen's) in the University. José Camilo Gallardo, warden of the University, mastered printing in a delusory fashion and produced some of the invitations and official announcements recorded in Medina's list of 1780-1811 imprints. However, neither Gallardo nor anyone else who may have operated the Haimhausen press printed any work necessitating a sustained effort.

In 1790 the Cabildo of Santiago de Chile requested permission from the king to establish a regular printing shop, but nothing came of the project. As late as 1803 it was necessary to have a *Reglamento del hospicio de pobres de la ciudad de Santiago* printed in Buenos Aires. When the struggle for Chilean independence formally began on 18 September 1810, it was clear that the absence of an effective printing shop could no longer be tolerated.

Printing was effectively introduced into Chile in 1811 by Mateo Arnaldo Hoevel, a native of Gothenburg (Sweden), a naturalized citizen of the United States. [6] Hoevel became the first foreigner to earn Chilean citizenship (1811), mayor of Santiago (1817) and founder of a distinguished Chilean family. With the cooperation of John R. Livingston of New York, Hoevel brought a press and three North American printers, Samuel Burr Johnston, [7] William H. Burbidge, and Simon Garrison. [8] He received 6,389 pesos from the government for the press, the cost of installation, and for various small arms that arrived with the press.

Two important early Chilean leaders claimed the credit for the introduction of the printing press into Chile in 1811. They are: General José Miguel Carrera[9]

(1785-1821), the country's first president, and Antonio José de Irisarri [10] (1786-1868). Still others suggest that it was introduced at the suggestion of the Chilean Congress. [11]

The first Chilean newspaper was *Aurora de Chile,* a weekly under the editorship of Fray Camilo Henríquez and over the imprint of "este Superior Gobierno." The first issue appeared on 13 February 1812. This newspaper had a prospectus, 46 ordinary numbers, two extraordinary numbers and a supplement in its first volume. The second volume contained twelve issues. It ceased publication on 1 April 1813. [12]

El Monitor Araucano, Chile's second newspaper, began publication on 6 April 1813 "En la Imprenta de Gobierno P. D. J. D. Gallardo." Three months later, on 29 June, Gallardo rented the press from the government and continued to hold it through the Spanish occupation (1814-1817). The *Monitor* ceased publication on 1 October 1814, and Gallardo, a royalist at heart, quickly found a modus vivendi with the new masters of Santiago. However, when the forces of San Martín and O'Higgins swept into northern Chile, Gallardo was stigmatized as an individual who was against the new regime; and the burden of maintaining Chile's typographical traditions passed to other hands. [13]

Notes

1. Guillermo Feliú Cruz, *Bibliografía histórica de la imprenta en Santiago de Chile 1818-1964* (Santiago de Chile, Talleres de la Editorial Nascimento, 1964) has brought together in one volume an elaborately annotated bibliography of material which deals with the history of printing in the Chilean capital.

2. While it would appear that historians of Chilean printing are mostly in agreement concerning the fact that Father Haimhausen introduced a printing press to Chile, they are by no means in agreement that it was used in Chile. Thus, Carlos H. Schabile, "Los origines de la imprenta en Chile," *El Mercurio* (Santiago), 6 November 1955, p. 4 (reproduced in Feliú Cruz, 59-60) notes that no imprint has survived even though the press, had it been used in Chile, would have existed there 19 years, *i.e.*, 1748-1767. He notes that Torre Revello has suggested that the Jesuit order might have had it moved to Ambato.

    Juan Canter, "El material impresor de Haimhausen y el origen del arte de imprimir en Chile y en Córdoba," *Segundo Congress internacional de historia de América* (Buenos Aires 1938), 5:78 feels that judgment concerning the introduction of printing to Chile by the Jesuits should be suspended until and unless examples of this press are found. Cantor sets forth the idea that this printing equipment was the origin of printing in Córdoba.

    Francisco A. Encina, *Historia de Chile desde la prehistoria hasta 1891* (Santiago, Editorial Nascimento, 1947) VI, 383 (see Feliú Cruz, pp. 72-73), states that after the expulsion of the Jesuits, the type and press passed to the University (*i.e.*, of San Felipe).

    Guillermo Furlong, *Orígenes del arte tipográfico en América especialmente en la República Argentina* (Buenos Aires, Editorial Huarpes, 1947), pp. 107-110 (see also Feliú Cruz, pp. 73-75), reproduces and agrees with much of the data provided by

Amunátegui Solar and notes that the Haimhausen press could not have gone to Córdoba for the Córdoba printing press that the Jesuits had in that city reached it through Buenos Aires and had come originally from Italy. Feliu. Cruz, pp. 75-76, cites Schaible's article to counter Furlong's statement that in 1754 there appeared in Chile a volume by Father Igancio Garzia entitled *Culto obsequioso y muy meritorio de el Alma de Christo.*

3. Schaible finds himself in complete disagreement with Domingo Amunátegui Solar, "La primera imprenta chilena se debió a la Compañía de Jesus," *Revista chilena de historia y geografía,* no. 78 (1933), 82-87.

4. Feliu Cruz, pp. 47-48.

5. Feliu Cruz, pp. 123-125.

6. The fullest discussion of Hoevel is Eugenio Pereira Salas, "Don Mateo Arnaldo Hoevel," *Revista chilena de historia y geografía,* no. 97 (1940), 57-93; summarized in Feliú Cruz, pp. 68-71.

7. Samuel B. Johnston's *Letters written during a residence of three years in Chile* (Erie, Pa., 1816), has appeared in several Spanish editions. José Toribio Medina translated it as *Cartes escritas durante una residencia de tres años en Chile...,* 139 (1916), 573-620, 140 (1917), 3-99. They were then published in Santiago-Valparaíso, Sociedad Imprenta-Litografía "Barcelona," 1917, 150 pp., pp. 3-17 are a biographical sketch of Johnston. This translation uncredited to Medina was published in the Biblioteca de la juventud hispanoamericana with the title *Diario de un tipógrafo*

yanqui en Chile y perú (Madrid, Editorial-América, 1919), with an introduction by Armando Donoso, which had first appeared as "Le que vió en Chile un tipográfo hace un siglo," *Zig-Zag*, no. 651 (11 Aug. 1917). See also Feliú Cruz, pp. 25, 55-56, 84-86, 88-89, 100, 107, 110.

8. For Burbidge and Garrison see Feliú Cruz, pp. 25, 85-86, 88-89, 110.

9. Feliu Cruz, pp. 7-8, 10-12, 22, 32, 53-54, 61, 84-85, 70, 101-103, 109 summarizes what various Chilean bibliographers and historians have written concerning Carrera and the introduction of printing into Chile. It is of interest that the article on Carrera in the *Encyclopedia Britanica*, IV, 960 merely credits him with having "inaugurated the first newspaper."

10. Feliú Cruz, pp. 7-8, 11, 22-23, 26, 34, 53, 62, 80, 82, 108, 121, 219, 141 summarize comments by Chilean bibliographers and historians on Irisarri's role in the introduction of printing to Chile.

11. Francisco A. Encina, *Resumen de la historia de Chile*, segunda edición (Santiago, Zig-Zag, 1956), I, 531.

12. Early studies on *La Aurora de Chile* are: Justo Molina, "Aurora de Chile," *La Estrella de Chile*, V (1873), 620-630, reprinted in *Zig-Zag*, no. 239 (18 Sept. 1909) and Daniel Riquelme, "La Aurora de Chile," *La Libertad Electoral*, no. 2248 (15 Feb. 1892), nos. 2256-2257 (24, 26, Feb. 1892). It was reprinted in 1903 (see Feliú Cruz, p. 41). Feliú Cruz contains numerous other references to this newspaper.

13. The *Monitor araucano* was reprinted in two volumes
as vols. 26-26 of the Colección de historiadores
y de documentos relativos a la independencia de
Chile, Santiago, 1914-1930. Vol. 1 was preceded
by a prologue by Thayer Ojeda; Vol. 2 has intro-
ductory material by Guillermo Feliú Cruz. Feliú
Cruz contains numerous bibliographical references
to this newspaper.

Chapter VIII

THE BEGINNING OF PRINTING IN
THE SPANISH ANTILLES

One might normally have assumed that printing
would have followed the course of the empire in Spanish
America and found its home in the Antilles. In reality
some of the oldest settlements were among the most
backward in acquiring presses. Santo Domingo and
Panamá knew nothing of printing before the nineteenth
century. It was not until 1807 that so ancient a
Caribbean community as San Juan de Puerto Rico
acquired a press. In the British Antilles and even in
British Guiana printing was well established in the
eighteenth century, expecially in Jamaica and Barbados.
Life was perhaps a bit too easy in most of the islands
to stimulate the cultivation of European crafts.

An exception was Cuba, the seat of a captain
general and always the richest and most significant of
the islands. The beginning of printing in Cuba has
been clouded by unfounded rumor and slipshod research
to which even such distinguished bibliographers as
Beristain de Souza and Antonio Bachiller y Morales
have contributed.

Thus, Ambrosio Valiente, *Tabla cronológica de los
sucesos ocurridos en la ciudad de Santiago de Cuba*[1]

(New York, 1853), p. 30 stated with no proof that printing was introduced in 1698. Beristain y Sousa claimed that the earliest Cuban imprint was dated 1707, [2] while Bachiller y Morales mentions an imprint of 1720. [3]

The first Cuban printer of whom we may speak with any certainty was Carlos Habré, [4] a foreigner, probably a Frenchman, of whom we know almost nothing. Bachiller emphasizes that Habré was a foreigner and notes that even the type was not that that ordinarily would have been used by a Spanish printer. He notes that among the type there was no ñ and he used an accented ú to express this sign that was unknown in the French language. He also used a profusion of circumflex accent marks and used capital letters to a greater degree than that demanded by the Spanish language of his time. It is Medina's opinion that Habré operated his press without the necessary official license and that the authorities simply tolerated his existence as a printer because they found him useful. [5]

His first known imprint is a *Tarifa general de precios de medicina* (Havana, 1723), reprinted in facsimile by Manuel Pérez Beato in his *La primera obra impresa en Cuba* (1936). The only other two books from Habré's press that we know for certain are the *Méritos que ha justificado y probado el Ldo. D. Antonio de Sousa* (1724) [6] and the *Rúbricas generales del breviario romano* (1727). [7] Until further proof is presented, we cannot accept any other Cuban imprints rumored to have existed before 1736.

We know little more about the life and work of Cuba's second printer, Francisco José de Paula. [8] On 4 June 1735 the Cabildo in Havana approved the issuance of a license to de Paula to print, possibly a recognition of the need of the new University of Havana (founded in 1734) for a printer. The first product of de Paula's press was, in fact, a university thesis by Juan Bautista Sollozo y Urrea, *Coelestis astrea* (1736).[9] Only two other publications of de Paula's are known, another thesis and an *Ordo recitandi officium divinum*, both dated 1741.[10] We know that de Paula received an appointment as printer to the Tribunal de Cruzada in 1741, and Bachiller says that de Paula sold his shop to Manual Azpeitia, from whom it later passed to Esteban José Boloña.

The third printer in Havana was Blas de los Olivos,[11] whose first imprint was a broadside entitled *Receta facil y provechosa contra dolores y llagas provenidas de humor galico* (1757),[12] the only copy known to Medina was that of the British Museum, whose copy was destroyed by enemy action in World War II. Blas de los Olivos' last imprint is dated 1777, and there are barely a dozen publications which may be definitely attributed to his press during the two decades of activity. Count de Recla, the island's captain general, attempted to make arrangements with Blas de los Olivos to print a "Gazeta", a "Mercurio mensual", and a "Guía de forasteros" with an almanac, but Madrid frowned on the project.[13] Indeed, on 20 January 1777 there was issued a royal *cédula* stating, "There shall be no printing house in the island, now or in the future, other than that of the Captaincy General".[14] Fortunately, this *cédula* never took effect, thanks to a succession of liberal governors, notably General Luis de las Casas, in the 1790's.

The printing house of the Cómputo eclesiástico began to serve the Cathedral and the various religious orders in 1762. From 1776 until the end of the century it used the more descriptive title of "Imprenta de la Curia Episcopal y Colegio Seminario de San Carlos". Its publications are, naturally, on religious themes.[15]

In 1781 the "Imprenta de la Capitanía General"[16]

began to function with the publication of a *Guía de forasteros* [17] and was the main printing house of Havana for the next three decades. In 1782 this shop began to issue the *Gazeta de la Habana,* [18] first under Diego de la Barrera and later under Francisco Seguí, who was associated in some way with the family of Blas de los Olivos. [19]

In 1787 Esteban José Boloña [20] initiated an important printing tradition in Havana when he began to print Ignacio José de Urrutia Montoya's *Teatro histórico jurídico, político militar de la Isla Fernandina de Cuba.* [21] This promising work ceased after the appearance of the first fascicle, but Urrutia's notes were undoubtedly used for his important *Compendio de memorias* published by the Imprenta de la Capitania General. [22] Despite his initial fragmentary effort, Boloña thrived, and he and his descendants were prominent printers in Havana until the middle of the nineteenth century. Boloña laid a sound foundation for the prosperity of his firm by securing official affiliation with the Inquisition in 1792 and the title of printer to the royal Navy in 1793. The imprints of the Boloña family were distinguished both for design and typography.

The last Havana printer who should be mentioned is Pedro Palma [23] (or Pedro Palmé or Pedro Nolasco Palmer), a sergeant invalided out of the army after two decades of service. He was first denied permission to print in view of the royal cédula of 1777, but the enlightened Governor Las Casas supported his request so vigorously that he was given permission to open his shop in 1791.

In 1790 the Imprenta de la Capitanía General [24] began to issue the noteworthy *Papel periódico de la Habana,* [25] the first bona fide magazine in Cuba. It was a major force in the intellectual life of the Habaneros for two decades and it was later known as *El aviso* and *Diario de la Habana.*

Histories of printing of colonial Spanish America give few details concerning the training of printers. The issue of 17 April 1800 of the *Papel periódico* is of interest, for it noted that the Real Sociedad Patriótico of Habana was willing to underwrite the training of two apprentices in the field. They were to be paid a monthly wage of ten pesos and were to be provided with clothing and board. The apprenticeship was to last three years. The boys were to be at least 14 years old. They should know how to read and write Spanish and should have a little Latin. They were to be examined from time to time to see how much progress they had made. [26]

The history of Cuba in the nineteenth century bears out only in part the bright promise of late eighteenth century Cuban publishing. The liberal governors of the period around the turn of the century were succeeded by small-minded men determined to hang on to Spain's last foothold in the western hemisphere at any cost. It was with the greatest difficulty that Cuban patriots were able to communicate effectively to fellow-countrymen; but men such as Blas de los Olivos, Las Casas, and Boloña had nevertheless an ineradicable tradition of a strong (although not free) press which was to be of the greatest inspiration to Cuban patriots in the culmination of events in the 1880's.

Notes

1. J. T. Medina, *La imprenta en La Habana (1707-1810)*, Santiago de Chile, Imprenta Elzeviriana, 1904, p. x.

118

2. Medina, p. xi.

3. Medina, p. xi, 4

4. Medina, pp. xii-xiii.

5. Medina, p. xiii.

6. Described by Medina, p. 5.

7. Described by Medina, pp. 7-9.

8. Medina, pp. xiii-xiv.

9. Described by Medina, p. 10.

10. Described by Medina, pp. 11-12.

11. Medina, pp. xiv-xviii.

12. Described by Medina, p. 15.

13. Medina, pp. xiv-xv.

14. Medina, p. xvi.

15. Medina, p. xvii.

16. Medina, p. xvii.

17. Described by Medina, p. 49.

18. Described by Medina, p. 52.

19. Medina, p. xviii.

20. Medina, p. xviii.

21. Described by Medina, p. 67.

22. Described by Medina, pp. 80-85.

23. Medina, p. xix-xx.

24. Medina, p. xvii.

25. Described and discussed by Medina, pp. 70-77.

26. Medina, pp. xxiii-xxv.

Ꞑriſtophorus Cabrera Burgenſis
ad lectorem ſacri baptiſmi minu
ſtrū: Dicolon Icaſtichon.

Si paucꝭ pnoſſe cupꝭ:uenerãde ſacerdos:
Ut baptizari quilibet Indus habet:
Quꝛ qꝛ p⁹ ōbēt ceu parua elemēta doceri:
Quicqd adultus iners ſcire tenetur itē:
Quaeꝗ ſient pſcis pꞃib⁹ ſancita:ꝓ orbem
Ut foret ad ritū tinct⁹ adultus aqua:
Utne dſpiciat (fors) tã ſublime Chariſma
Indulus ignarus terꝗ quaterꝗ miſer:
Hūc māib⁹ vſa:tere:plege:dilige libꝛum:
Wilmin⁹ obſcurū:nil magis eſt nitidum.
Siplicꞇ docteꝗ ōdit modo Uaſc⁹ acut⁹
Addo Quiroga me⁹ pſul abunde pius.
Sigula ppēdens nihil ide regrere poſſis:
Si placet⁾ oē legas ordine diſpoſitum.
Ne videare (caue) ſacris ignauus abuti:
Sis decet ad uigilās:mittito deſidiam.
Nēpe bonū nihil uꞇqꝗ fecerit oſcitabūdus.
Difficile eſt pulchrū:dictitat Antiqtas.
Sed ſatꝫ e:qd me remorarꝫ pluribꞌ:inqs.
Sit ſatis: ꞇ facias quod precor:atꝗ uale.

Recto of the first leaf of *Manual de Adultos* issued by
Juan Pablos on 13 December 1540, the first surviving
Mexican imprint.

121

Title-page of *Doctrina breve*, the first major work printed by Juan Pablos (1543).

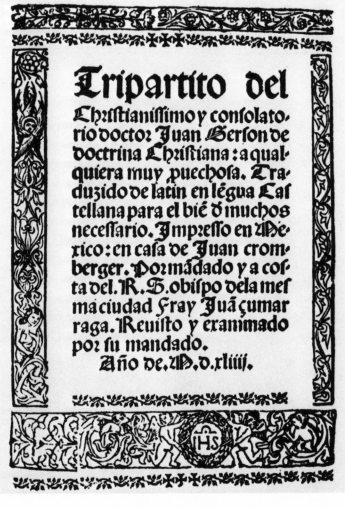

Tripartito del
Christianissimo y consolatorio doctor Juan Gerson de
doctrina Christiana : a qual-
quiera muy puechosa. Tra-
duzido de latin en légua Cas
tellana para el bié ð muchos
necessario. Impresso en Ade-
rico : en casa de Juan cromberger. Por mádado y a costa del. R. S. obispo dela mes
ma ciudad Fray Juá çumar
raga. Reuisto y exammado
por su mandado.
Año de. AD. D. xliiij.

Title-page of Juan Pablos' edition of Johannes Gerson's
Tripartito (1544).

123

Aue Mariagratia

plena dominus tecū.

The first full-page wood engraving in an American
book, in Pablos' edition of Gerson's *Tripartito* (1554).

¶ Summario cõpédioso delas quẽtas de plata y oro q̃ en los reynos del Piru son necessarias a los mercáderes:y todo genero de tratantes. Cõ algunas reglas tocantes al Arithmetica.

�֍ Fecho por Juan Diez freyle. ✖

Juan Diéz Freile, *Summario compendioso*, printed by Pablos in 1556, the first mathematical book printed in America.

Title-page of Fray Alonso de la Vera Cruz, *Phisica speculatio*, printed by Juan Pablos in 1557.

Title-page of Pablos' edition of Fray Alonso de la Vera Cruz' *Recognitio summularum* (1554), probably the first Roman type used in the New World.

¶ **Arte de la lengua Mexi**
cana y Caſtellana ,compueſta por el muy Rç
uerendo padre fray Alonſo de Molina de la orden de Señor
ſant Franciſco.

¶ En Mexico en caſa de Pedro Ocharte. 1571

A philological publication by Pedro Ocharte just before
his incarceration by the Holy Office. The engraving of
the stigmata of St. Francis was frequently used in
sixteenth century Mexican books.

DOCTRINA

CHRISTIANA, EN LENGVA ME

xicana muy neceffaria : en la qual
fe contienen todos los princi
pales myfterios de nue-
ftra Sancta Fee ca-
tholica .:.

*COMPVESTA POR EL MVY REVE-
rendo Padre Fray Alonfo de Molina, de la orden
del gloriofo Padre Sant Francifco.*

CON PRIVILEGIO.
En Mexico, En cafa de Pedro Ocharte.
M.D.LXXVIII,

Pedro Ocharte resumed work as an independent printer
in 1578 with Fray Alonso de Molina's *Doctrina christiana*
and Fray Juan de Córdoba's *Arte en lengua zapoteca.*

ARTE Y DICTIO

NARIO : CON OTRAS

Obras, en lengua Michuacana. Cõpuesto por
el muy. R. P Fray Iuan Baptista de Lagu
nas, Prædicador, Guardian de sanct
Francisco, de la ciudad de Gua-
yangareo, y Diffinidor dela
Prouincia de Mechua-
can, y de Xalisco.
DIRIGIDAS AL MVY YLLV. Y. R.
señor Doctor dõ Antonio Morales ã Molina, Caua
llero de la ordê de Sãctiago, obispo meritissimo q̃ fue
de Mechuacã, y agora de Tlaxcala, del cõs. de su. M.

EN MEXICO,
En casa de Pedro Balli.
1574.

Title-page of the first recorded imprint of Pedro Balli,
Mexico's fourth printer.

130

SERMONARIO
EN LENGVA
MEXICANA, DONDE SE CON-
TIENE (POR EL ORDEN DEL MISSAL
NVEVO ROMANO,) DOS SERMONES
en todas las Dominicas y Festiuidades principales de todo el año:
y otro en las Fiestas de los Sanctos, con sus vidas, y Comunes.

CON VN CATHECISMO EN LENGVA MEXICANA
y Española, con el Calendario. Compuesto por el reuerendo padre
Fray Iuan de la Annunciacion, Subprior del monaste-
rio de sant Augustin de Mexico.

DIRIGIDO AL MVY REVERENDO PADRE MAE-
stro fray Alonso de la vera cruz, Prouincial de la orden de los
Hermitaños de sant Augustin, en esta nueua España.

EN MEXICO, por Antonio Ricardo. M. D. L X X V I I.
Esta tassado en papel en   pesos.

Title-page of one of the first books printed by Antonio
Ricardo in Mexico (1577).

131

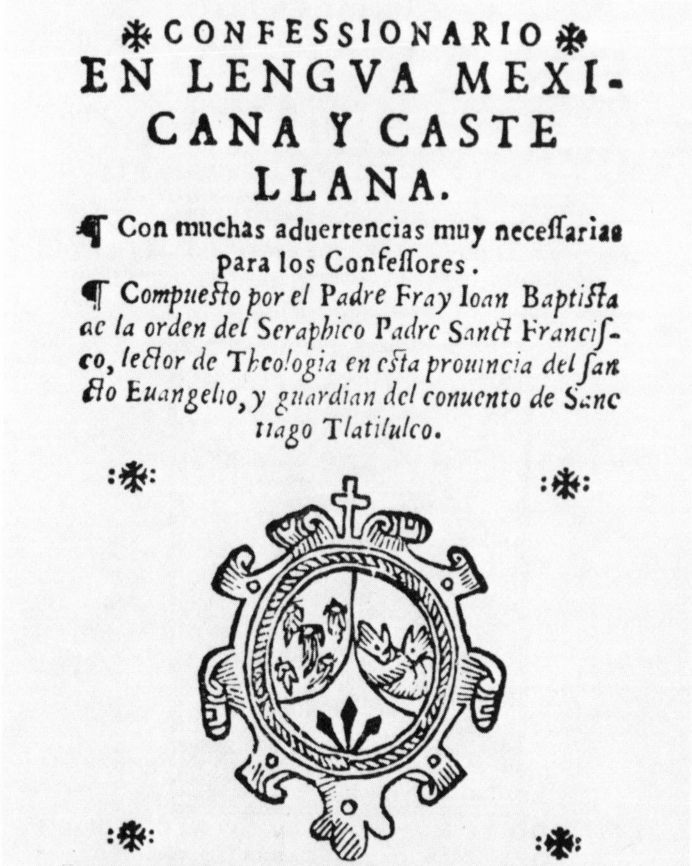

❋ CONFESSIONARIO ❋
EN LENGVA MEXI-
CANA Y CASTE
LLANA.

¶ Con muchas aduertencias muy neceſſarias para los Confeſſores.

¶ *Compueſto por el Padre Fray Ioan Baptiſta de la orden del Seraphico Padre Sanct Franciſco, lector de Theologia en eſta prouincia del ſancto Euangelio, y guardian del conuento de Sanctiago Tlatilulco.*

❋ CON PRIVILEGIO. ❋

¶ En Sanctiago Tlatilulco, Por Melchior Ocharte. Año de. 1599.

Title-page of the first imprint of Melchor (or Melchior) Ocharte, the seventh printer of Mexico.

The explanation of a chronological error in several works. This mutilated copy of Ricardo's *Doctrina christiana* of 1584 in the Bartolomé Mitre Collection in Buenos Aires has the Roman numeral date of 1583 in manuscript despite the M.D. LXXXIII in the imprint. In some copies the last I in the Roman is broken and seems to have been filled in in this copy.

DOCTRINA
CHRISTIANA,
Y CATECISMO PARA INSTRVC-
cion de los Indios, y de las de mas perso-
nas, que han de fer enfeñadas en nueftra fanlla Fe.
CON VN CONFESSIONARIO, Y OTRAS COSAS
neceſſarias para los que doɛtrinan, que ſe con
tienen en la pagina ſiguiente.
COMPVESTO POR AVCTORIDAD DEL CONCILIO
Frouincial, que ſe celebro en la Ciudad de los Reyes, el año de 1583.
Y por la miſma traduzido en las dos lenguas generales,
de eſte Reyno, Quichua, y Aymara.

℞ DVLCE TVVM NOSTRO
NOMINE NOSTRA SALVS.
SCRIBA SIN PECTORE NOMEN
NAMQVE TVO CONSTAT
IHS

Impreſſo con licencia dela Real Audiencia, en la
Ciudad de los Reyes, por Antonio Ricardo primero
Impreſſor en eſtos Reynos del Piru.
AÑO DE M. D. LXXXIII; AÑOS.
Eſta taſſado vn Real por cada pliego, en papel.

The second Lima imprint and the first major work
issued in Peru, the *Doctrina christiana* printed by
Antonio Ricardo in 1584.

134

huápas payta , vi-
ac ſiruincanchic-
Amen Ieſus.

machita áropa
chañaſſataqui
cácana. Amen

Fin del Catecifmo mayor.

This engraving which appears at the end of the
catechism in Ricardo's *Doctrina christiana* of 1584,
was one of many that travelled vast distances in
colonial America.

DOCTRINA
CHRISTIANA.

P Or la feñal de la fanᘓa Cruz, de nueſtros ene-
migos, libranos feñor Dios nueſtro.
En el nombre del Padre, y del Hijo, y del Spiritu
Sanᘓo. Amen.

QVICHVA.

S Anᘓa cruzpa vnan-
chanraycu, aucaycu
cunamanta, quifpi-
chihuaycu Dios apuy-
cu.
Yayap, Churip, Spi-
ritu Sanᘓop futimpi.
Amen Iefus.

AYMARA.

S Anᘓa cruzana vnan
chapaláycu. aucana
cahàta nanaca qui-
fpijta, nanàcana Dios
ápuha.
Anquina, Yocànfa,
Spiritu fanᘓónfa furipa
na. Amen Iefus.

EL PATER NOSTER.

P Adre nueſtro, que eſtas en los cielos, fanᘓifica
do fea el tu nombre. Venga a nos el tu reyno.
Hagafe tu voluntad, afsi en la tierra, como en
el cielo. El pan nueſtro de cada dia, danos lo oy. Y
perdona nos nueſtras deudas, afsi como notorros
A   las

Page from Ricardo's *Doctrina christiana* of 1584 showing
the arrangement of Quechua, Aymara and Spanish texts.

GAZETA

DE LIMA

QUE CONTIENE LAS NOTI.

cias de efta Capital defde 25. de Septiembre
hafta fin de Octubre de 1745.

L A ESCASEZ QUE SE EXPERIMENTA EN ESTA CA-
pital, de aquellas novedades, que todo bien confiderado caben
en la Gazeta, es tanta à vezes, que no permite el formarla
con fuficiente cuerpo; principalmente defpues de los repetidos
avios que nos han venido, tanto de adentro, como de fuera, de def-
terrar de ella algunos acaecimentos de poco, ó ningun importe para
las Provincias, aunque de algun valor, para los que viven en efta Cor-
te, y que por efto mifmo los faben mas á tiempo; y de abreviar otras
noti.

The *Gazeta de Lima* was the first American newspaper
to be published regularly south of Mexico.

137

Title-page of *De la differencia entre lo temporal y eterno*, the first surviving Paraguayan imprint.

INSTRVCCION
PRACTICA
PARA

Ordenar Santamente la vida ; que
ofrece El P. Antonio Garriga de
la Compañia de Iefus.
Como brebe memorial, y recuerdo
à los que hazen los exerccios efpi-
rituales de S. Ignacio de lo
yola Fundador de la
mifma Com-
pañia.

En Loreto, con licencia de los
Superiores en la Imprenta de
la Compañia

Año de 1713

Paraguayan book of 1713 showing imprint of Loreto.

MANUALE

Ad *vſum*

Patrum   Societatis

I E S V.

Qui in Reductionibus

PARAQVARIÆ

verſantur

Ex Rituali Romano
ac Toletano ...
decerptum

Anno Domini MDCCXXI
Superiorum permiſsu

Laureti typis P. P. Societatis IESV.

Paraguayan book of 1727 showing imprint of Loreto

ARTE

DE LA LENGUA GUARANI

POR EL P. ANTONIO RUIZ

DE

Montoya

DE LA COMPAÑIA

DE

JESUS

Con los Escolios Anotaciones
y Apendices

DEL P. PAULO RESTIVO

de la misma Compañia
Sacados de los papeles

DEL P. SIMON BANDINI

y de otros.

En el Pueblo de S. MARIA La Mayor

El AÑO de el Señor MDCCXXIV

Paraguayan book of 1724 showing imprint of Santa María La Mayor.

EXPLICACION
DE EL
CATECHISMO
EN LENGUA GUARANI
POR NICOLAS YAPUGUAI
CON DIRECCION
DEL P. PAULO RESTIVO
DE LA COMPAÑIA
DE
JESUS

En el Pueblo de S. MARIA La Mayor.
AÑO DE MDCCXXIV

Paraguayan book of 1724 showing imprint of Santa María
La Mayor.

REGLAS,
Y CONSTITVCIONES,
QVE HAN DE GVARDAR
los Colegiales del Colegio Real de
N. S. de Monferrate.

1   COMO la puerta para entrar à la Divina Sabiduria, fea el temor de Dios, pongan toda fee, cuidado en temer de ofenderle, teniendo continuo en fu coraçon fu Santa Ley.

2   El blanco de fus eftudios fea el fervir, y complacer à la Mageftad de Dios, ratificando à menudo efta intencion, y pidiendo los govierne, y enderece para tan alto fin; y afsi al entrar en el Colegio Confeffaràn, y Comulga-

First page of text of *Reglas y constitvciones que han de guardar los Colegiales del Colegio Real de N.S. de Monserrate* (Córdoba, 1766-1767).

143

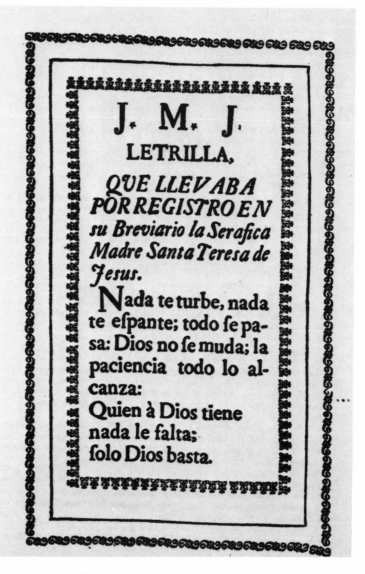

J. M. J.

LETRILLA,

QUE LLEVABA POR REGISTRO EN su Breviario la Serafica Madre Santa Teresa de Jesus.

Nada te turbe, nada te eſpante; todo ſe paſa: Dios no ſe muda; la paciencia todo lo alcanza: Quien à Dios tiene nada le falta; ſolo Dios basta.

Probably the first Buenos Aires imprint from the press of the Niños Expósitos in 1780.

✠

Y NFORMADO del desarreglo, y abusos con que se exercita la Medicina, Cirujia, y la Pharmacia, y Phlebotomia á ellas anexa, con especialidad en las Provincias distantes de esta, Capital, he resuelto por áhora establecer, y crear en ella un Tribunal de Proto-medicato, como lo hay en las Ciudades de Lima, y Mexico, con las mismas facultades, prerrogativas, y exempciones, para que por este medio, que tanto se conforma con las Leyes, se corrija, y extirpe el desorden : y hè venido en elegir, y nombrar al Doctor Don Miguel Gorman, en quien concurren las partes, y Calidades necesarias por Proto-Medico, y Alcalde mayor de todos los respectivos Profesores á efecto de que desde luego proceda, y providencie lo conveniente ál expresado fin, que consulta à la salud publica.

Y como no seria ásequible, si á sus mandamientos no seles diese en los Pueblos, y distritos de estas Provincias el cumplimiento, que à toda Carta de Justicia es necesario, hè dispuesto consiguientemente , participarlo à V.S. para que en esta inteligencia haga reconocer en todas las Ciudades, Villas, y Pueblos de su jurisdiccion, y V.S. reconosca al mencionado Don Miguel de Gorman por Proto-Medico del Tribunal Real del Proto-medicato nuevamente establecido, y creado en esta Capital, embiando à sus Cabildos, y respectivos Gefes Copia de esta mi orden para que teniendolo todos entendido, igualmente den en lo succesivo el fomento, auxilio, y ayuda, que necesiten las Providencias de dicho Proto-Medico relativas al expresado fin; siendo por ahora lo que mas deve llamar la atencion de todos, y con especialidad la de V.S. no permitir desde el recivo de esta en adelante en ningun Pueblo de Españoles de essa Provincia el que alguno entre á exercer de nuevo la Medicina, Cirujia, Pharmacia, y Phlebotomia, sin que primero confte por recaudos bastantes, y en debida forma haver sido examinado por el Real Proto-medicato de esta Ciudad, merecido la aprobacion de sus examinadores, y hallarse en su consequencia autorizado para exercerlas; haciendo al mismo tiempo, que todos los que al presente pasan plaza de Medicos, Cirujanos, Boticarios, y Sangradores presenten dentro de un breve termino sus titulos ante las Justicias de los respectivos Pueblos, de los quales se sacará una Copia, y los Originales se remitiran al Tribunal del Real Proto-medicato, para que viftos, y examinados en èl se provea lo conveniente àcerca de su uso, y à los que no los presentasen dentro de el termino referido se les prohivirà bajo las penas establecidas por Leyes efte exercicio, no permitiendoseles en adelante sin que primero hagan los eftudios, y practica necesaria, y ocurran à examinarse, y solicitar la competente aprovacion, y licencia, dandome V.S. aviso en primera oportunidad de haverlo asi cumplido en todo, y de pronto el recibo de esta.

Dios guarde à V. m. a. Buenos-ayres. 16 de Noviembre de 1780.

Juan Joseph de Vertiz

The second Buenos Aires imprint, a broadside (134 x 235 mm.) dated 1780. Twenty-three copies are together in the Archive General de la Nación, Buenos Aires (Impressos, t.2), and Furlong records others, some not now located.

145

EXTRACTO DE LAS

Noticias recibidas de Europa por la via de Portugal.

GAZETA DE LISBOA

1. DE MAYO 1781.

Madrid 24. de Abril.

Abemos por las Cartas de los Comandantes Generales de Mar, y Tierra del bloqueo de Gibraltar con fecha de 12. del corriente, que en el mismo dia llegò à aquella Plaza el Comboy *Ingles*, compuesto de 28. Navios de Linea, 9. de los quales eran de 3. puentes, 10. Fragatas, y 97. Embarcaciones de Transporte. Habiendo dado los Generales anticipadamente sus órdenes para hacer lo que fuese mas idóneo para daño de los Enemigos, el de Mar luego que las Embarcaciones empezaron à embocar el *Estrecho*, embiò a' Mayor General *D. Ventura Moren* con 1ª. Lanchas armadas con artilleria, y 4. con bombas mandadas por Oficiales à *Punta Carnero*, las que fondeandose en linea, salieron al encuentro con tal intrepidez, resolucion, y método, que haciendo fuego contra una Fragata, y dos Navios, que venian por cabeza del Comboy, los obligaron à responder con toda su artilleria, durando este ataque 2. horas, hasta que las dichas Lanchas se retiraron por haber refrescado el viento.

One of the news-sheets printed in Buenos Aires in 1781.

146

CLARISSIMI VIRI

D.D.IGNATII
DUARTII ET
QUIROSII,
COLLEGII MONSSERRA-
TENSIS CORDUBÆ IN
AMERICA CONDITORIS,

LAUDATIONES
QUINQUE,
QUAS
EIDEM COLLEGIO REGIO
BARNABAS ECHANIQUIUS O.D.

Corduba Tucumanorum Anno. MDCCLXVI,
Typis Collegii R. Monfferratenfis.

Title-page of *Laudationes* (1766) in honor of Dr. Ignacio
Duarte y Quirós, the first surviving imprint of Córdoba
de Tucumán.

HISTORIA
REAL
SAGRADA,
LVZ
DE PRINCIPES.
Y
SVBDITOS.

Dedicada

AL PRINCIPE NVESTRO SEÑOR.

POR

EL ILLVSTRISSIMO, Y REVERENDISSIMO
Don Iuan de Palafox, y Mendoça, Obiſpo de la Puebla de los
Angeles, del Conſejo de ſu Mageſtad.

CON LICENCIA,

En la Ciudad de los Angeles, Por *Francisco Robledo*, Impreſſor del Secreto del Santo Oficio.
Año de 1643.

Title-page of the fourth surviving imprint from Puebla
de los Angeles, Bishop Juan de Palafox y Mendoza's
Historia real sagrada (1643).

HISTORIA DE LA
SINGVLAR VIDA, DE EL VE=
NERABLE HERMANO FRAY CHRISTO,
val de Molina Religioso Lego de la Orden de N. P.
San Augustin,

Hijo de el illustrissimo Convento de Nuestra Señora de Gra=
cia de la misma Orden; de la Ciudad de la Puebla de los
Angeles donde recivió el habito, y murió.

ESCRITA POR EL PADRE LECTOR Fr. NICOLAS
Ponze de Leon, Religioso de la misma Orden. Año de 1686.

DEDICADA AL CAPITAN DIEGO DE AN=
drada Peralta, Alcalde Ordinario, que fué en la muy Noble
Ciudad de la Puebla de los Angeles; y Sobrino de el Vene=
rable Hermano.

CON LICENCIA
En la Puebla de los Angeles por Diego Fernandez de Leon. Año de 1686.
Vendense en su Tienda en la esquina de la Plaça en la Calle de Cholula

Title-page of life of Cristóbal de Molina, printed in
1686 by Diego Fernández de León, the most important
of the Puebla printers of the seventeenth century.

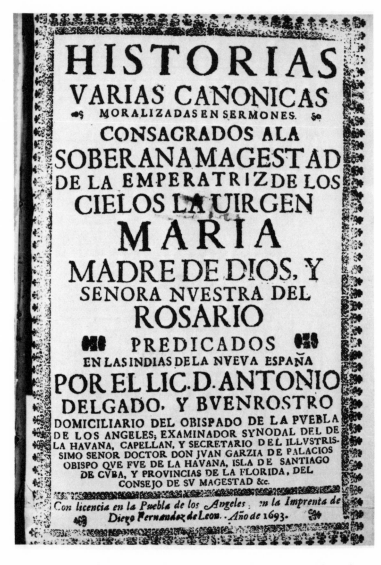

HISTORIAS
VARIAS CANONICAS
MORALIZADAS EN SERMONES.
CONSAGRADOS ALA
SOBERANA MAGESTAD
DE LA EMPERATRIZ DE LOS
CIELOS LA UIRGEN
MARIA
MADRE DE DIOS, Y
SENORA NVESTRA DEL
ROSARIO
PREDICADOS
EN LAS INDIAS DE LA NVEVA ESPAÑA
POR EL LIC. D. ANTONIO
DELGADO, Y BVENROSTRO
DOMICILIARIO DEL OBISPADO DE LA PVEBLA
DE LOS ANGELES; EXAMINADOR SYNODAL DEL DE
LA HAVANA, CAPELLAN, Y SECRETARIO DEL ILLVSTRIS-
SIMO SENOR DOCTOR DON JVAN GARZIA DE PALACIOS
OBISPO QVE FVE DE LA HAVANA, ISLA DE SANTIAGO
DE CVBA, Y PROVINCIAS DE LA FLORIDA, DEL
CONSEJO DE SV MAGESTAD &c.

Con licencia en la Puebla de los Angeles, en la Imprenta de
Diego Fernandez de Leon. Año de 1693.

Title-page of Antonio Delgado y Buenrostro, *Historias varias canónicas*, printed by Diego Fernández de León in Puebla in 1693.

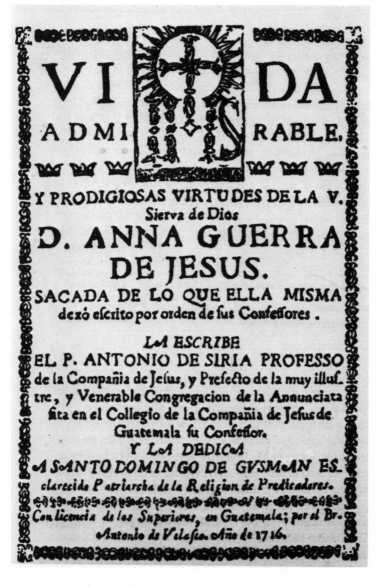

VI DA
ADMI RABLE,

Y PRODIGIOSAS VIRTUDES DE LA V.
Sierva de Dios
D. ANNA GUERRA
DE JESUS.
SACADA DE LO QUE ELLA MISMA
dexó escrito por orden de sus Confessores.

LA ESCRIBE
EL P. ANTONIO DE SIRIA PROFESSO
de la Compañia de Jesus, y Prefecto de la muy illus-
tre, y Venerable Congregacion de la Annunciata
sita en el Collegio de la Compañia de Jesus de
Guatemala su Confessor.
Y LA DEDICA
A SANTO DOMINGO DE GVSMAN ES-
clarecido Patriarcha de la Religion de Predicadores.

Con licencia de los Superiores, en Guatemala; por el Br.
Antonio de Velasco. Año de 1716.

Title-page of the life of Ana Guerra printed in Guatemala
by Antonio Velasco in 1716.

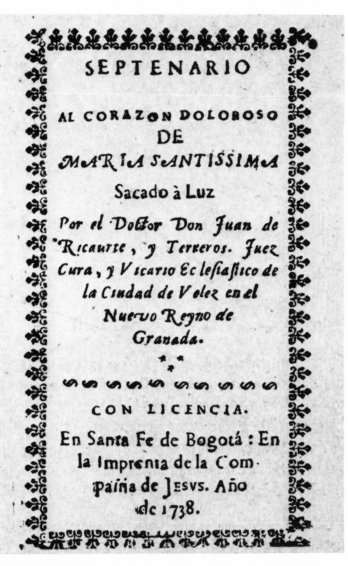

SEPTENARIO

AL CORAZON DOLOROSO
DE
MARIA SANTISSIMA
Sacado à Luz
Por el Doctor Don Juan de
Ricaurte, y Terreros. Juez
Cura, y Vicario Ec lesiastico de
la Ciudad de Velez en el
Nuevo Reyno de
Granada.

CON LICENCIA.

En Santa Fe de Bogotá: En
la Imprenta de la Com-
pañia de Jesvs. Año
de 1738.

Title-page of the *Septenario* printed by the Jesuits in Bogotá in 1738, the first surviving imprint from New Granada.

152

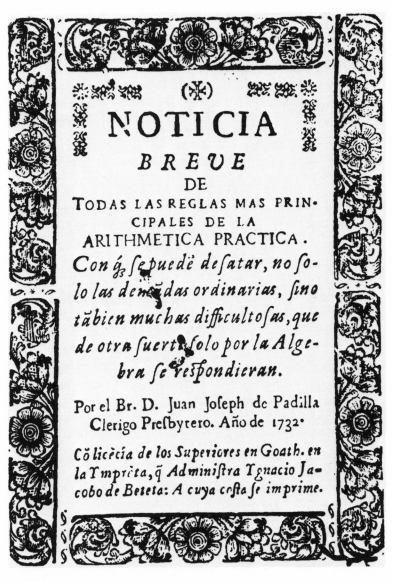

NOTICIA
BREVE
DE
TODAS LAS REGLAS MAS PRIN-
CIPALES DE LA
ARITHMETICA PRACTICA.

Con ģ₃ ſepuedē deſatar, no ſolo las demādas ordinarias, ſino
tābien muchas difficultoſas, que
de otra ſuerte ſolo por la Algebra ſe reſpondieran.

Por el Br. D. Juan Joſeph de Padilla
Clerigo Preſbytero. Año de 1732·

Cō licēcia de los Superiores en Goath. en
la Ymprēta, ģ Adminiſtra Ygnacio Jacobo de Beteta: A cuya coſta ſe imprime.

Title-page of an arithmetic printed in Guatemala in
1732 by Ignacio Jacobo de Beteta, the only known
imprint from this minor press.

1739

AFFECTUOSA
NOVENA
DE LA SANTISSIMA
Virgen Maria,

EN SV MILAGROSA ADVOCACION

DE LA PEñA.

QVE DEDICA A SV SANTISSIMA
Imagen,

SU MAS INDIGNO
SIERVO EL
BACHILLER BALTHA-
far de Meſſa, Capellan de
ſu Hermita.

En Santa Fè de Bogotà: En la
Imprenta de la Compañia de
JESVS Año 1739.

Title-page of the *Novena* printed in Bogotá by the
Jesuits in 1739, recorded by Enrique Posada as the
second imprint of this city.

PIISSIMA
ERGA
DEI GENITRICEM
DEVOTIO
Ad impetrandam gratiam
pro articulo mortis.
*Ex Seraphico Doctore Divo
Bonaventura deprompta.*
Cura, & folicitudine fervorum
JEfu, Mariæ, & Jofeph.
Cum variis Orationibus ante, &
poft Confeffion. & Commun.
Cum Licentia.

HAMBATI,
Typis, Soc. JEfu. Anno 1755.

A 1

Title-page of St. Bonaventure's *Piisima erga Dei genetricem devotio* (Ambato, 1755), the first known Ecuadorean imprint.

155

LA ESCLAVITUD MAS HONROSA,
EXERCICIO
QVE CADA DIA PVEDEN
praĚicar los devotos Efclavos
EN OBSEQUIO
DE LA GRAN REYNA
DE CIELOS, Y TIERRA
MARIA SS.ᴹᴬ
DEL CARMEN.
A mayor Gloria de Dios,
Honra de tan Gran Madre, Con-
fuelo, y provecho de las
Almas.

HAMBATI, typis Soc JESU
Anni 1759.

A 10

Title-page of a book printed in 1759, the last year of the Jesuit press in Ambato.

PONTIFICALE
ROMANUM
CLEMENTIS VIII. primum,.

nunc denuò

URBANI PAPÆ VIII.

AUTHORITATE RECOGNITUM

CLEMENTIS
PAPÆ VIII.

CONSTITUTIO

Super Pontificalis Editionem.

Cum Facultate Superiorum.

HAMBATI . typis Societatis JEfu.
Anno 1755.

A 2

Title-page of the second Ambato imprint of 1755.

)(✠)(

DESCRIPCION
EXACTA
DE LA PROVINCIA
DE
BENEZUELA,

POR
D. Joseph Luis de Cisneros.

DEDICALA
A UN INCOGNITO AMIGO SUYO.

· ·

IMPRESSO EN VALENCIA,
Año de M. DCCLXIV.

Title-page of the much debated description of Venezuela by José Luís de Cisneros, said by Medina to have been printed in Nueva Valencia, Venezuela, in 1764.

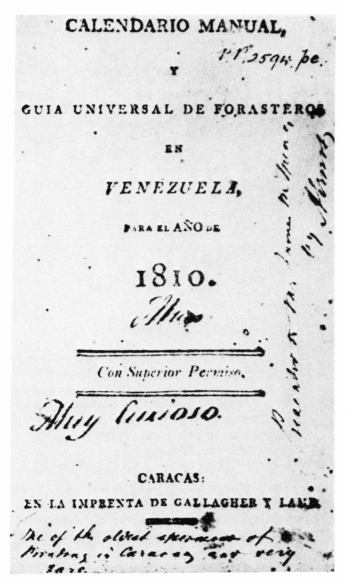

CALENDARIO MANUAL,

Y

GUIA UNIVERSAL DE FORASTEROS

EN

VENEZUELA,

PARA EL AÑO DE

1810.

Con Superior Permiso.

CARACAS:

EN LA IMPRENTA DE GALLAGHER Y LAMB

Title-page of the first non-serial Caracas imprint, the *Calendario manual* of 1810.

159

CLARISSIMI VIRI
D. D. IGNATII DUARTII ET QUIROSII

LAUDATIO I.

NESSE MAJORUM NOBILITATI
vim suam, quæ non finat degenerare mino-
res ab avita gloria, is neget unus, qui & ig-
nobilis ipse sit, nullisque majoribus, nec magni
illud vatis audierit unquam:

Fortes creantur fortibus, & bonis.
Nec imbellem feroces
Progenerant aquilæ columbam. (1)

Certè heroicis illis temporibus sola commendatio vir-
tutis distinxit è plebe nobiles. Nam siquis arte quadam
dicendi & eloquentiâ dispersos homines, & vagantes more
belluarum in unum locum conjunxerat; siquis ingenio, & pru-

B   den-

─────────────────────────────

(1) *Horat. Lib. 4. Od. 4.*

First page of text of *Laudationes* (Córdoba, 1766).

PERSONAL NAME INDEX

165

SHORT TITLE INDEX

167